COUNTDOWN TO SUPER BOWL

How the 1968–1969 New York Jets Delivered on Joe Namath's Guarantee to Win It All

Dave Anderson

SPORTS
PUBLISHING

Published by arrangement with Random House, a division of Penguin Random House LLC.

Sports Publishing books may be purchased in bulk at special discounts for sales promotion, corporate gifts, fund-raising, or educational purposes. Special editions can also be created to specifications. For details, contact the Special Sales Department, Sports Publishing, 307 West 36th Street, 11th Floor, New York, NY 10018 or sportspubbooks@skyhorsepublishing.com.

Sports Publishing® is a registered trademark of Skyhorse Publishing, Inc.®, a Delaware corporation.

Visit our website at www.sportspubbooks.com.

10 9 8 7 6 5 4 3 2

Library of Congress Cataloging-in-Publication Data is available on file.

Cover design by Tom Lau
Cover photo credit Associated Press

ISBN: 978-1-68358-264-9
Ebook ISBN: 978-1-68358-265-6

Printed in the United States of America

THE ANATOMY OF AN UPSET

Ten days before the New York Jets were to face the Baltimore Colts in the Super Bowl, Jimmy the Greek (the man who sets the odds from coast-to-coast) called it: "The number is 17, the Colts by 17."

Ten days before the New York Jets were to face the Baltimore Colts in the Super Bowl, Joe Willie Namath called it: "We're going to win; I'll guarantee it."

One of them was going to be wrong—very wrong, and Jimmy the Greek was almost always right. But not this time . . .

How a brash young football star proved a master odds-maker wrong, is the story of a super-upset that changed the course of pro football history.

"Superb . . . cinematic . . . the best of the new books inspired by the Jets' victory over the Colts, a game that provided rich symbolism for the victories of a new league and of a controversial quarterback."—*The New York Times*

To Maureen
who made the last two days the best

CONTENTS

INTRODUCTION

This isn't a book so much as it's an 11-day time capsule of how Joe Namath and the New York Jets won Super Bowl III, a stunning 16–7 upset of the Baltimore Colts half a century ago in an America that was aflame. Protestors of the Vietnam War disrupted the Democratic Convention in Chicago. Before the Jets swept to an 11–3 record in the 1968 season Dr. Martin Luther King was assassinated in Memphis on April 4, and Bobby Kennedy was assassinated in Los Angeles on June 5. At the Olympics in Mexico City, Tommie Smith, the gold medalist in the 200-meter dash, and John Carlos, the bronze medalist, each raised a black-gloved "black power" fist as the national anthem played. Richard Nixon was elected president.

And on the 12th day of 1969, the Jets won the Super Bowl. The Jets from that "other league," the nine-year-old American Football League that proved it was as good as the champions of the National Football League that had been around for nearly half a century, the Jets with a shaggy-haired quarterback that dared to "guarantee" a victory.

That's why Super Bowl III has endured as arguably the most memorable of more than 50 Super Bowls. Old-timers remember Vince Lombardi's Green Bay Packers winning the first Super Bowl and also the second. Fans of other Super Bowl winners remember those particular games, but just about every pro football fan remembers Joe Namath and the Jets.

That's what prompted this rare reprint 50 years later of *Countdown*. And here are its day-to-day details as I observed them or learned about them as the *New York Times* reporter, who covered the Jets throughout the 1968 season, the AFL championship game, and Super Bowl III.

Sadly for the Jets' generations of frustrated fans over the last half-century, the team has yet to return to the Super Bowl, but they wasted four opportunities in the AFC championship game. The 1982 team, with Richard Todd at quarterback, lost on a soggy field in Miami, 14–0. The 1998 team, with Vinny Testaverde at quarterback, lost in Denver, 23–10. The 2009 team, with Mark Sanchez at quarterback, lost in Indianapolis, 30–19, and the 2010 team, again with Sanchez at quarterback, lost in Pittsburgh, 24–19.

At least the 1968 Jets advanced to Super Bowl III and won it. The Detroit Lions, the Cleveland Browns, the Jacksonville Jaguars, and the Houston Texans have yet to get to the Super Bowl at all.

And surely the Jets someday will return to the Super Bowl. Someday.

—Dave Anderson

THURSDAY, JANUARY 2
"Chicken Ain't Nothin' But a Bird"

The quarterback lifted the top of the small white box. Inside, on a patch of cotton, gleamed a gold brooch, its diamonds sparkling.

"It's for my mother," Joe Namath said. "It's her Christmas present. We had to practice that day, and I wasn't able to get home to give it to her, but she's coming down next weekend for the game."

"How many diamonds are in it?" asked John Free, the New York Jets' traveling secretary.

"I don't know, I didn't even count 'em," Namath said. "I just fell in love with it when I saw it."

"It looks like twelve," Free said. "Here, let me count how many."

Crouching in the aisle of the chartered Northeast Airlines jet, Free silently counted the diamonds.

"Twelve," he said. "The same as your number."

"Twelve diamonds," Joe Namath said, with a sly smile. "My number is twelve, and we're playing them on the twelfth. This has got to be an omen."

Most people believed the New York Jets would need much more than an omen.

At this moment, shortly after six o'clock on Thursday evening, January 2, 1969, the champions of the American Football League were on their way to Fort Lauderdale, Florida, where they would be lodged while they prepared for the Super Bowl game in Miami with the Baltimore Colts, the National Football League champions. As their yellow Boeing 727, its wing lights flashing, droned above the clouds, the Jets were considered by most of the outside world to be the only lambs ever led to slaughter at an altitude of 35,000 feet.

The previous Sunday the Jets had needed to rally in the final quarter for a 27–23 victory over the Oakland Raiders in the AFL championship game. That same day the Colts had thrashed the Cleveland Browns, 34–0, for the NFL championship.

But there was no atmosphere of impending doom among those on the Jets' charter. The players had gathered at Shea Stadium at noon to review the films of the AFL championship game and to listen to their head coach, Weeb Ewbank, warn them *not to* provoke the Colts with any inflammatory statements.

"Let me do all the talking about the Colts," the coach had commanded.

Later in the afternoon, they had regrouped in the Northeast Airlines terminal at Kennedy International Airport. Relaxing on a soft beige chair in a private waiting lounge there, Larry Grantham, the experienced linebacker who calls the defensive signals, had disclosed the team's approach to the game.

"Joe will get us points," Grantham said, meaning the quarterback, "and it's up to the defense to make sure whatever points he gets us are enough."

Not far away, Curley Johnson, the punter and the team's humorist, had established the attitude as he poured some Johnnie Walker Red Label scotch over the ice cubes in a big, tall glass.

"Chicken ain't nothin' but a bird," Curley said, "and this ain't nothin' but another football game."

"Where'd you get that?" asked Paul "Rocky" Rochester, a beefy defensive tackle. "You make that up?"

"One of my uncles, A. R. Johnson, down home in Dallas, it's one of his sayings. He's a car salesman, and if he don't sell a car, he'll say that. Chicken ain't nothin' but a bird, and this ain't nothin' but another football game."

"And the Colts," said Rochester, "ain't nothin' but another football team."

"Nothin' but a bird," Johnson said, sipping his scotch. "Ain't nothin' but a bird."

When he boarded the plane, he had repeated softly, "Chicken ain't nothin' but a bird, nothin' but a bird," as he strolled down the long aisle to the last row of seats. All the players who heard him knew what he meant, because they had heard him saying it all season. Now, under the hum of the jets as the 727 cruised toward Florida, Johnson played gin rummy with Rochester as their teammates traveled as they always do—some playing cards, some reading, some chatting, some sleeping, and some worrying about the next game as they stared through the windows into the black sky.

"Those hand-fighters bother me," Randy Rasmussen was saying. "They're tough on me."

The 23-year-old right guard would have to prevent Billy Ray Smith, the Colts' seasoned 33-year-old defensive tackle, from getting to Joe Namath, and even now, with the game ten days away, he was worrying about his responsibility.

"He's a big, rough guy," Rasmussen said. "He's been around a real long time."

But most of the players appeared relaxed. On this trip, a few wives were accompanying their husbands, and a few small children also were along. Bob Talamini, the left guard, and his brunette wife, Charlene, had their four children with them and 2-year-old Tina Marie was being displayed by John Schmitt, the big bear of a center. Cornell Gordon, a defensive back and a habitual card player, surveyed his poker hand while 1-year-old Cornell, Jr., sat on his lap, a nippled bottle hanging from his mouth.

"That's a cute son you've got there," somebody said.

"He's wearin' me out," his father replied, tenderly.

That afternoon in Baltimore, the Colts had worked out briefly, secure in their role as a 17-point betting favorite, the widest point spread in the three-year history of the Super Bowl series. Their only concern was the condition of the swollen left ankle of Bubba Smith, their 295-pound defensive end.

"I'll be all right for the game," Bubba had said.

And in his office at Memorial Stadium, the Colt coach, Don Shula, had agreed.

"He'll be all right. We won't have any excuses."

While the Jets' charter passed over the Virginia coastline, another jet zoomed up above the gaudy strip of hotels in Las Vegas, Nevada. One of its occupants, Jimmy "The Greek" Snyder, was suffering from acute abdominal pains and was on his way to College Hospital in Santa Barbara, California, for an examination.

Of the millions who had watched the Jets and the Colts on television the previous Sunday, the most provocative judgment of their comparable skills had been made by Jimmy "The Greek," tall, husky, black-haired, 49 years old.

With the rolled, show-biz collar of his soft blue shirt propped high above his black cashmere sports jacket, Jimmy The Greek is as much a fixture in Las Vegas as the gambling casinos. Whenever he appears at The Sands or Caesars Palace or The Dunes, a parking attendant might ask, "What's good, Jimmy?" Or inside, a hotel executive might say, "Give me a winner, Jimmy," because Dimetrios Synodinos, as he was christened in Steubenville, Ohio, establishes the pro football betting line each week for most of the nation.

And that Sunday, after viewing the Jets and the Colts, he announced, "The number is 17, the Colts by 17."

The next day, in his Information Unlimited public-relations office, he explained how he arrived at the point-spread that, for betting purposes, was supposed to equalize the game. The Colts would have to out-score the Jets by more than 17 points if those interested in betting on the Colts were to win their wager.

"They sold me with their defense," Jimmy was saying in his gravel voice. "The AFL is improving each year, but the Jets have a tiger by the tail."

In its ninth year of operation, the AFL had not yet outgrown its label as the "other" league. During the previous summer, the AFL teams had compiled a 13–10 won-lost record in pre-season exhibition games with NFL teams, but most people forgot that. Instead, they remembered that the Green Bay Packers of the NFL had defeated the AFL representatives decisively in each of the two previous Super Bowl games. Each time the Packers had upheld Jimmy The Greek's point spread. As a 14-point choice over the Kansas City Chiefs after the 1966 season, the Packers won, 35–10. The following year, as a 15-point choice over Oakland, the Packers won, 33–14.

"And the Colts," said Jimmy The Greek, "have the greatest defensive team in football history, better than the Packers."

In forming a point spread, Jimmy The Greek puts an emphasis on defense. He awards X amount of points for such specific factors as overall team speed, the front four linemen on defense, the linebackers, and the defensive backs. He then analyzes the quarterbacks, the pass-receivers, the running backs, and the field-goal kickers. He also considers a few intangibles, such as a team's mental attitude and its coach.

"I gave the Colts 12 points on defense alone—4 to their front four, 4 to the linebackers, and 4 to their defensive backs," he said. "They're the first team I've ever given more than 3 points in any defensive category."

He had been awed by the Colts' defense in a shutout of the Browns. Including that game, the Colts had blanked four opponents in winning their last ten games. During that span, they had permitted only six touchdowns—three by the Los Angeles Rams in a 28–24 victory that had no bearing on the Coastal Division race and two by the Minnesota Vikings after the Colts were well in command of the Western Conference title game, which they won, 24–14.

"On offense," the oddsmaker said, "the quarterbacks come out even. I rate Namath a 5-point quarterback. He and Sonny Jurgensen are the only ones I rate that high. Earl Morrall is worth 3 points, but having Johnny Unitas behind him makes the quarter-backing even. Unitas can't throw the long one much anymore, but if he has to come in, he'll call the right plays, and he can throw short. Imagine having a Unitas available as a backup.

"The receivers are even, so are the field-goal kickers. That kid Jim Turner had a great year for the Jets, but Lou Michaels has more experience, so they come out even.

"In overall team speed, they're even, but I think the Colt running backs deserve a 2-point edge. Tom Matte is fantastic, and Jerry Hill is a great blocker. So that's 14 points—12 on defense, 2 for the running backs. Add 3 for the intangibles like the NFL mystique and Don Shula's coaching. The Jets have good coaching. Walt Michaels is a great defensive coach, and Weeb Ewbank is solid, but I have to give the Colts the edge.

"But the big thing is their defense. I like Namath and his wide receivers, but the Jets won't be able to establish a running game. The Colts held Leroy Kelly of the Browns to 28 yards in thirteen carries, and he *led* the NFL the past two years. If the Colts can stop Kelly, then Matt Snell and Emerson Boozer won't be able to do much. Without a running game, the Colt pass-rush will be hurrying Namath. The Colts just look too good defensively.

"Until they blanked the Browns, I was figuring on the Colts by about 12," Jimmy The Greek said, "but now it's got to be 17, and if you want to bet without a spread, it's 7 to 1."

The oracle had spoken. The point-spread had been established, and it had flared into a controversy. Not enough, claimed those who believed in NFL superiority. Ridiculous, claimed those who had seen Joe Namath dissect opponents and the Jet defensive unit rule its league. But at the moment, Jimmy "The Greek" Snyder, being flown across the Sierra Nevada mountains, was more concerned with the persistent pain in his abdomen.

On the Jets' charter, the pilot's voice blared through the intercom system.

"The temperature in Fort Lauderdale," he announced, "is seventy-two and clear. In case you've forgotten, it was twenty-six when we left New York."

Up front, Weeb Ewbank, the pudgy coach, smiled at Clive Rush, his offense aide.

"That's what I like to hear," Ewbank said. "That's why we came down early."

Below, lights twinkled in Georgia, as Joe Namath, wearing a blue turtleneck shirt and maroon corduroy slacks, sat on the left side of the aisle in the second row of the economy section. Traditionally, the wider, more comfortable first-class seats on a charter are reserved for the Jet coaches, club officials, and newsmen. The meal is the same for all. Players sometimes stand and chat with a coach or a newsman in the first-class section, but in the unspoken caste system, no player is invited to sit there, not even Joe Namath.

In another unspoken rule, the quarterback has a seat reserved for him: second row, left side of the aisle.

The aisle is important. It makes it easier for him to extend his tender right knee, scarred twice by surgery. But on this flight, the seat in front of him was empty. He had folded its backrest forward, and he had propped his right foot, in a brown suede boot, onto it.

Now, as he swirled the ice in his plastic cup of Johnnie Walker Red, he raised a dark eyebrow at the mention of the 17-point betting line.

"I didn't know we were that bad a football team," he said, sarcastically. Then he became serious. "If we were allowed to bet, I'd bet a hundred thousand on this one. It's going to be a challenge for us, but it's going to be a challenge for them, too. I might sound like I'm boasting and bragging, and I am. Ask anybody who's played against us in our league. The Colts are good, but *we're* good, too."

The Colts had compiled a 15–1 record, including their championship victory, while the Jets were 12–3 overall.

"But when the Colts lost to the Browns at mid-season," Namath continued, "they didn't get beat by any powerhouse. I'm not going to take what I read about their defense. I'm going to go with what the one-eyed monster shows me."

The one-eyed monster is the projector that shows game films.

"The one-eyed monster doesn't lie. He shows it like it is."

The previous Sunday, in the midst of the confusion and the champagne of the AFL championship, Namath had rated Daryle Lamonica, the Oakland quarterback, as "better" than Earl Morrall, the surprising savior of the Colts—an opinion that had stung not only the Colts but NFL loyalists everywhere.

"I said it, and I meant it," Namath was saying now, "Lamonica is better."

His bold opinion was considered to be a psychological lift for the Colts.

"But if they need newspaper clippings to get up for a game," Namath continued, "they're in trouble. And if they're football players, they know Lamonica can throw better than Morrall. I watch quarterbacks, I watch what they do."

He had seen the Colts twice on television—against the Packers and the Vikings—when the Jets weren't scheduled.

"You put Babe Parilli with Baltimore instead of Morrall, and Baltimore might've been better. Babe throws better than Morrall. I might be prejudiced about that, because Babe is with us. But I believe it."

Parilli had been discarded by the NFL a decade earlier, but after several seasons as a star with the Boston Patriots of the AFL, he had been obtained by the Jets as a backup quarterback.

"If you put any pro quarterback on our team, only a few wouldn't be third-string. That's my opinion. I don't care how people value my opinion, but I value it very highly, especially when I'm talking about football. And all the talk about the NFL being a better league. There are *more* teams in the NFL, so they should have more good teams. But you put their good teams and our good teams together, or their bad teams and our bad teams together, it's 50-50, flip a coin. And we've got better quarterbacks in our league—John Hadl, Lamonica, myself, Bob Griese."

Hadl directs the San Diego Chargers while Griese is with the Miami Dolphins.

"I read where some NFL guy joked about Lamonica and me throwing nearly 100 passes last Sunday," he said, sipping his scotch. "And we threw 97, but what's so terrible about that? How many NFL teams have a quarterback who could complete as many passes to their wide receivers as we do? In our league, we throw much more to our wide receivers than they do to theirs. I completed 49 percent of my passes this season, but I could've completed 80 percent if I dropped the ball off to my backs like they do in their league."

During the 14-game season, Namath had completed 187 of 380 passes for a 49.2 percentage, 3,147 yards, and 17 touchdowns.

"For wide receivers, the Jets have the best," he said. "George Sauer has the best moves, nobody can cover him one-on-one, and Don Maynard is the smartest. And when a quarterback has wide receivers that good, he *should* throw to them."

All around him, the other players had finished their dinner—a shrimp cocktail, steak, peas, mashed potatoes, cheesecake, and coffee. Now, one of the stewardesses approached with a tray and lowered it toward the quarterback's lap.

"No, thanks, nothing for me," Namath said.

Instead, he lifted the tray into the row behind him where John Schmitt, the 245-pound center, took it.

"But he's had dinner," the stewardess protested.

"He's a growing boy," Namath said, with a wink.

In his fourth season, the quarterback appeared to have matured in AFL competition, notably after both the Buffalo Bills and the Denver Broncos intercepted five of his passes to achieve upset victories early in the schedule. Of the remaining nine games in the regular season, the Jets won eight. In their only loss during that span, they were leading, 32–29, against Oakland with sixty-five seconds to play. In a finish that created a national furor when a production of "Heidi" replaced the game on most TV sets throughout the nation, the Raiders produced two touchdowns within nine seconds for a 43–32 victory. During those nine games, only five of Namath's 208 passes were intercepted, a remarkable 2.4 percentage that indicated his maturity as a quarterback.

"I don't feel matured, if that's the word," he was saying now, as the charter droned across the Florida border. "People might think I've matured now but that's because we've been winning. And the reason we've been winning is defense."

Not entirely. Another compelling reason was that Namath directed a winning touchdown in the final two minutes of two victories and positioned a winning field goal by Jim Turner in the final four minutes of another game. But perhaps his most important performance occurred in the season opener. He guided the offensive unit to a 70-yard, ball-control drive against the Kansas City Chiefs in the final six minutes to preserve a 20–19 victory. The day before, he had been elected captain of the offensive unit, a mandate from his teammates. After the dramatic triumph, while everybody waited that night for the equipment to be loaded onto the charter flight to New York, he strolled into the first-class section to rehash the successful strategy with Weeb Ewbank.

"That's the first time Joe's ever come up front like that to talk after a game," Clive Rush, the offense coach, would whisper later. "Maybe the captaincy has made him a leader."

Two weeks later, the Buffalo Bills intercepted five of Namath's passes, returning three of them for touchdowns in a 37–35 upset, the only victory of the season for the lowly Bills. In the locker room, Namath shook his head sadly and said, "I just wasn't reacting good." Several days later he joked about how he had discussed the Bills with Ray Abruzzese, an ex-Jet defensive back who is his roommate in an apartment with the llama rug on the East Side of Manhattan.

"Before the game, we couldn't figure out how the Bills could score quickly," Namath recalled, "but when I got back Sunday night, Ray said, 'Now I know how the Bills can score quick.'"

When the Denver Broncos also produced five interceptions, depriving the Jets of another expected triumph, Namath did not make excuses or jokes. After that game, he appeared at his locker with a serious, almost stern expression.

"I ain't saying nothin'," he announced, "except that I stink."

After that, his aroma changed. So did his style. He didn't throw a touchdown pass during the next four games, but the Jets won all of them. At the time, he bridled at the suggestion that he had retooled his thinking. He claimed that the absence of touchdown passes was merely a matter of circumstances, but now, as he headed toward the Super Bowl showdown, he disclosed how the interceptions had changed him.

"I disciplined myself as to throwing the ball," he said, swirling the ice in his cup. "I was overcautious at times. I remembered an old rule that the only way to win is to keep from losing."

In the AFL championship game, another interception led to the touchdown that put Oakland ahead, 23–20, midway in the final quarter. The 25-year-old quarterback suddenly was confronted with the most critical situation in his celebrated career. Unless he guided the Jets to another score, he would be thought of as over-rated, and worse, as overpaid. As a rookie in 1965, he had received a contract that, with salary and various bonus arrangements, was worth $427,000. Prior to the 1968 season, he had signed a new three-year contract that was presumed to be worth even more.

Now, with the seconds flashing on the Shea Stadium scoreboard, he had to justify his earnings.

Provided with decent field position at his own 32-yard line after Earl Christy's kickoff return, Namath connected with split end Sauer on a square-out pattern at the left sideline for a first down at the 42. On the next play, he flung a long arching pass at his flanker, Maynard, who had a step on Oakland's George Atkinson, a rookie cornerback. Maynard was expecting the pass over his left shoulder, but in the swirling wind, it floated down to his right. Clutching the ball at the 10-yard line, Maynard was dragged down at the 6.

Considering that Namath had retreated to nearly the 30-yard line, plus the added distance across the field toward the sideline, he threw that pass about 75 yards in the air.

On the next play, he obligated himself to a roll-out to his left, with halfback Bill Mathis the intended receiver on a flare pass. But the strong Raider rush disrupted Namath's plan. Aware that Mathis was covered, he glanced at Sauer, then at tight end Pete Lammons, but both were covered. His eyes fanning to the right, he searched for Maynard and found him in the end zone with several Raiders surrounding him. With the quick release of an archer's bow, Namath arrowed the ball toward his flanker.

"I heard that ball hum," fullback Matt Snell would say later. "I *heard* that ball go by me."

The next thing Snell heard was the roar from 62,627 spectators. Maynard had caught the pass, the force of it knocking him to his knees in the cold, brown dirt of the end zone. With three passes accumulating a total of 68 yards, Namath had produced a touchdown in fifty-five seconds. And that touchdown would provide the Jets with the AFL championship. Suddenly, despite his exorbitant initial cost of $427,000, he was a bargain.

"But any player has to be lucky," he was saying now on the plane. "You have to have some luck."

He lifted his right leg, flexed the knee slightly, and gently replaced it on the folded seat.

"You take Tank here," he said, nodding across the aisle at place-kicker Jim Turner, "suppose he had to have an operation on his right knee when he was playing quarterback at Utah State. If he did, he wouldn't be kicking now. I was lucky because I was trained good by my brothers, Bob and Frank, and I've had good coaches. Larry Bruno, my coach at Beaver Falls High School, he was terrific. He had eleven guys go on scholarship to college, eleven guys from *one* team. And to go from a coach like that to Coach Bear Bryant at Alabama, a kid has to be lucky. He made me feel proud to be a part of his team. I learned a lot from Coach Bryant.

"And then coming here, with Weeb, was lucky for me. But until this season, I don't think I really appreciated Weeb."

As a rookie, he certainly didn't. Once, in an exhibition game in the rain, Ewbank, with 196 pounds on his round 5-foot 7-inch frame, was knocked by a cluster of players into the mud. When he tried to get up, he slipped and plopped into the mud again. Out on the field, in the huddle before the next play, Namath was watching Ewbank flop around in the mud.

"Get up, you little butterball," the quarterback was saying quietly, amusing his teammates. "Get up so I can use the same play again."

Namath didn't repeat the "play," but the incident was significant. After having played under Paul "Bear" Bryant, tall and handsome, Namath was unable to develop an immediate respect for his new coach, short and fat. Even during his third season, Namath ignored a warning from Ewbank about the passing attack. The previous Sunday, the Jets had not played because of a bye in the schedule, and now, in the days before a December game with the Denver Broncos, rain had limited their practice sessions.

"Our timing is going to be off," Ewbank kept worrying. "Our timing won't be right. We're in trouble."

Namath laughed. *Weeb's crazy*, he later acknowledged thinking. *How can our timing be off when we've been practicing for four months?*

"But in the game," Namath confessed later, "I had Lammons wide open and missed him. My timing [was] off."

He had five passes intercepted that day, too, and the Jets were upset by the Broncos. The defeat proved to be the one-game difference that gave the Houston Oilers the Eastern Division title.

Now, on the plane, Namath was thinking of the 1968 day when he was chatting with trainer Jeff Snedeker.

"Jeff always opens up the locker room," the quarterback said, "and one day when he got there at eight o'clock, Weeb already was there, taking a whirlpool bath. He had a sore muscle or something, but he was there early so he wouldn't have to waste time in the whirlpool later on. I mean Weeb's an old man, he's 61, and he was in the locker room before eight o'clock in the morning. And the day we came back from San Diego, six weeks ago, after just about clinching our division, Weeb and the coaches got off the plane at seven in the morning, and they went straight to the stadium. They could have taken a break, nobody gets a good sleep on a plane, but they went right to work looking at films for our next game."

Above, the seat-belt sign flashed red. The charter was nearing Fort Lauderdale International Airport.

"I've had my disagreements with Weeb, I probably always will. I'm that kind. Like last Sunday, after we won the championship, there's a league rule that you're not supposed to have champagne in the locker room. So the club had it in the back room where it wouldn't be so obvious, twenty-five cases of it. But I told Weeb to break it out, that all of us were three-times-seven, and that I'd pay the fine out of my pocket.

"And later, Mr. Woodard, Milt Woodard, the president of the league, came over to talk to me about it, and I told him it's a stupid rule, that all of us were three-times-seven and that it was the biggest day of our lives and that we deserved champagne.

"Mr. Woodard tried to tell me that it was bad for the image of football, that it was bad for the kids to see it. But you know what the real image of football is? It's brutality. Why don't they tell the kids like it is? Tell the kids that this guy is trying to hurt that guy and knock him out of the football game. Or show them the letters I get from people who hope some guy cripples me because of my mustache."

Namath had grown a Fu Manchu mustache that flourished for several weeks before he accepted $10,000 to shave it off with a Schick electric razor for a TV commercial.

"Some of those letters," Joe Namath was saying now, clicking his seat belt and gently lowering his right leg into the aisle, "some of those letters I read for entertainment because those people are sick. Or maybe I'm the sick one, but I'm happy the way I'm sick."

When the 727 rolled to a stop, two silver buses with red-and-blue trim were waiting nearby. One by one, the players descended into the warm air, many of them carrying plastic clothes bags. Their luggage was being plopped onto a truck for separate delivery, along with the 2,500 pounds of football equipment that had traveled in the baggage compartment. Nearly all the players were on the buses when Joe Namath appeared atop the ramp, his eyes squinting into the bright TV lights.

"Oh, there he is," squealed a teenage girl. "I've just got to kiss him."

But she didn't, because the quarterback was hustled off to a TV interview.

Soon the buses, escorted by four motorcycle policemen with their sirens wailing, were on their way to Galt Ocean Mile Hotel, where the Green Bay Packers had stayed a year earlier. Up Route A1A, past the piers of chartered fishing boats on the left, past the moonlit beach with swaying palm trees on the right, the buses sped through the city, slowing but never stopping for the red lights as the policemen waved sidestreet traffic to a halt. The atmosphere dazzled some of the players.

"Yes, sir," said Jim Turner, the place-kicker. "We've come a long way from the Polo Grounds."

For four years, before their transfer to Shea Stadium in 1964, the Jets and their predecessors, the Titans, had played at the old Polo Grounds, a gray and grimy stadium. The Titans had performed in poverty. During the 1962 season, the Titans had more unpaid bills than players. Once, the laundry man refused to leave a supply of locker-room towels unless the team's bill, which had been ignored by club president Harry Wismer, was paid.

"Here," said George Sauer, Sr., reaching into his pocket, "consider yourself paid."

Sauer was the general manager, the only front-office man to survive the transition to the Jets when David "Sonny" Werblin organized a group that purchased the franchise for one million dollars. The coach, Clyde "Bulldog" Turner, was not retained. Although he once was an All-NFL center with the Chicago Bears two decades earlier, he had not kept up with the scientific advances of football. He occasionally diagrammed plays on the sideline during a game. Another time he was chalking a play known as "60 Banana" on the blackboard when he suddenly turned to one of his assistant coaches. "How do you spell banana?" he asked. Turner and his predecessor, Sammy Baugh, had to put up with the eccentricities of Wismer, the meddling president. Wismer negotiated the national television contract that helped to launch the AFL, and for that reason, he deserved commendation. But his inability to meet his expenses nearly destroyed the New York franchise as well as the whole league. Some of the checks he did write bounced higher than the Polo Grounds roof.

Once, when the players' salary checks were repeatedly delayed, the athletes called a strike. After they missed three days of practice, the AFL office guaranteed the paychecks. With only a quick Saturday workout behind them, the Titans defeated the Buffalo Bills the next day, a tribute to the players' devotion to duty. Three of those players—Larry Grantham, Don Maynard, and Bill Mathis—who had spanned the era from the 1960 Titans through the 1968 qualifiers for the Super Bowl, remembered how, in the Wismer era, they had sometimes played before fewer people than those who stood on the sidewalk now on Atlantic Avenue *in* Fort Lauderdale to watch the Jets zoom by.

"In 1963," Clive Rush was saying to Jim Turner, "we had three teams—one going, one coming, and one playing."

The buses slowed and turned into the wide cement driveway at the Galt Ocean Mile Hotel, its bright entrance glowing in a soft yellow light, its foliage a deep green, so unlike the winter grayness of New York that the team had escaped. Beyond the oak-paneled lobby, palm trees surrounded the shimmering green water of the swimming pool. And out over the beach, with its surf thudding onto the sand, the moon shone high in the black sky.

"This," said one of the players, enjoying the scene, "is the way to get ready for a football game."

Soon the lobby was empty. After getting settled in their rooms, some players stayed there, watching television, or going to sleep early or, like the Talamini family, which had adjoining rooms—one for the parents, one for their four small children—waiting for another crib to be delivered. Other players reappeared in the lobby on the way into the hotel bar, the Rum House, featuring Blackie Nelson and the Personalities, or across the street to the orange-roofed Howard Johnson's for a sandwich, or out for a few drinks somewhere else.

No curfew had been installed, and none would be until Tuesday night.

"Let them have their fun," Weeb Ewbank had confided to his coaches. "They deserve it, and I don't want to regiment them now anyway. But on Tuesday, we'll begin to clamp down."

FRIDAY, JANUARY 3
57 More Minutes to Work With

Overnight, clouds had swooped across the southern part of Florida. When Joe Namath awoke in the Governor's Suite of the Galt, the beach outside his top-floor balcony was gray with mist.

The year before, when the Packers were here, Vince Lombardi had occupied this suite, labeled as room 534.

Wherever the Jets go, Namath requests a suite for himself and his roommate, safetyman Jim Hudson. The two players share the cost above the price of a regular double room, which the Jets pay for. But now, as Hudson slept late, Namath had been contacted by two members of the Federal Bureau of Investigation.

"Routine," one of them said.

Several weeks earlier, a man had threatened the quarterback in a telephone call to Bachelors III, Namath's New York restaurant. That man, the FBI believed, was in the Miami area, but after a brief interrogation, the agents departed.

"His room's in a good spot," one of them said.

"That's right," the other agreed. "His balcony faces the beach, not the pool like the others do. If that guy is going to take a shot at him, he can't hide in the palm trees around the pool. He's got to stand out there on the beach to get a look at him, and if he does that, he'll never get away."

Later, when Namath arrived downstairs, he stopped at the registration desk.

"I'd like a receipt for this," he said. "I want to put it in your safety box."

And the quarterback handed over the small white box with the diamond brooch.

Out at Fort Lauderdale Stadium, with its pastel pink-and-green grandstand and its royal palm trees towering beyond the black outfield fence, Bill Hampton, the 39-year-old equipment manager, stood in the spacious locker room used by the New York Yankees during spring training.

"Start the offense on the left," Hampton, tall and friendly, was saying, "and put the defense on the right."

Hampton and two helpers, Herb Norman and Mickey Rendine, began to place the individual green equipment bags containing a helmet, shoes, and various protective pads at the open plywood lockers. The grouping was by position—quarterbacks, running backs, linemen, and pass-receivers on the left; backs, linebackers, and linemen on the right. There were forty active players and three players—flanker Harvey Nairn and defensive linemen Karl Henke and Ray Hayes— who could be activated if an injury should disable one of the forty-man squad. In addition, Mike Stromberg, a rookie linebacker who had required mid-season knee surgery, was along. Among other duties, he would operate the phone to the coaches' booth during the game.

"Leave an empty locker between Namath and Turner," said Hampton, "because Joe will need room for the writers."

At Shea Stadium, the quarterback dresses between Babe Parilli, the 38-year-old backup quarterback, and Jim Turner, the place-kicker, who is an emergency quarterback. In front of Namath's locker there is a huge pillar that results in a mob scene when newsmen crowd around, a continual inconvenience to Turner and Parilli.

"Turner's always moaning about it," Hampton continued. "We got the room here to keep him happy."

When the individual equipment was stored in the lockers, they began to unpack the big green trunks. First, the one containing the practice uniforms and sweat suits. Then the one with extra equipment, such as helmets, face-masks, pads, and chin-straps. Then the one with the coaches' gear. Then the one used by trainer Jeff Snedeker for his medical supplies. But the fifth trunk remained locked. That one contained the white game uniforms.

"And the footballs?" Hampton was asking now. "We had two boxes of new footballs."

"I put them in the coaches' room," Norman said, "so that nobody would get at them."

Two bags of used footballs had been brought along. In addition, in the event of cool weather or rain, there were sideline jackets and raincoats. When the unpacking was completed, one of the stadium workers strolled in.

"That locker 12," he said, "that's Namath's locker, isn't it?"

"That's right," Hampton said.

"You got him in Mickey Mantle's locker," the workman said. "I bet you did that on purpose."

"I didn't know that was Mantle's locker," Hampton said, truly surprised. "Honest, I didn't."

Outside the cashier's booth in the Galt lobby, John Free was holding a tall stack of ten-dollar bills.

"How much money you got there in your hand, John Free?" asked Larry Grantham, the linebacker.

"Seven thousand, one hundred, and fifty dollars," the traveling secretary whispered. "The meal money for everybody the whole time we're here."

"You ever hear about guys getting hit on the head carrying a lot of money?" Grantham asked.

Free smiled patiently. At the age of 51, he had become the perfect foil for the players who teased him, who blamed him, who enjoyed him. He had become acquainted with Weeb Ewbank in Baltimore, where he was a sales manager for a building supply firm, and when Ewbank reorganized the Jets, he wanted his trusted friend, John Free, with him. And now, as the narrow-faced traveling secretary looked past Grantham, he noticed Jeff Richardson, a reserve offensive lineman, in the lobby.

"Jeff Richardson," he called. "I want you to be my deputy sheriff."

After a mock deputization ceremony, the 6-foot 3-inch, 250-pound lineman escorted Free to his room, where he counted out one hundred ten dollars for each of the sixty-five people in the Jets' official party and slipped the money into separate envelopes.

The previous Sunday, in the spontaneous celebration that had followed the winning of the AFL championship, Weeb Ewbank had been lifted onto the shoulders of his players. Photographers had recorded the moment with Ewbank's face contorted in tears, presumably tears of joy. But now, as he moved through the Galt's dining room, with the pool and patio beyond its high glass wall, the pudgy little coach was hobbling on a gray cane.

"What happened?" somebody asked.

"Remember when the players put me on their shoulders," he said. "Well, some little kid came along and swung on my right leg. It really irritated the hip joint."

"Then they were not tears of joy?"

"They were tears, period," he said.

He knew the difference. Wilbur Charles Ewbank, whose nickname developed when his brother was unable to pronounce his name properly, is the only man to have coached championship teams in both the AFL and the NFL. He had coached the Colts to the NFL title in 1958 when Johnny Unitas directed the memorable 23–17 sudden-death victory over the New York Giants, and again in

1959, but in between his years of glory, there were years of toil and trouble.

Following the 1962 season, when the Colts dropped to a 7–7 record, Carroll Rosenbloom, the team's president, dismissed Ewbank and hired Don Shula.

Several weeks later, in early 1963, David "Sonny" Werblin organized a group that purchased the bankrupt New York Titans. Werblin's first moves were to appoint Ewbank as general manager and coach and to rename the team the Jets.

"I had a five-year plan in Baltimore," Ewbank said then, thinking back to when he joined the Colts in 1954, "and I don't see why we can't build a winner here in five years."

When the Eastern Division title failed to materialize in the 1967 season, he was castigated by many critics for failing to fulfill his prophecy. The critics refused to take into account the knee surgery that season for Matt Snell and Emerson Boozer, the team's two best running backs. Despite the wail of the critics, Werblin decided to retain Ewbank for the final season of his three-year contract. Suddenly, in a stock shuffle, Werblin was out. The new owners approached Vince Lombardi of the Packers and Al Davis of the Raiders, but in the end, Ewbank remained. Prior to the 1968 season, the new president, Phil Iselin, made it clear that Ewbank would not be rehired unless the Jets attained at least the divisional title.

Ironically, the absence of Werblin made it easier for Ewbank to take true command of the team for the first time.

Werblin, the show business impresario who had signed Joe Namath to his celebrated contract, had been involved with every facet of the club, perhaps too much so. He not only was the president, but he thought nothing of overruling Ewbank in his general manager's role. Werblin saved the AFL when he signed Namath, but he became personally involved with the quarterback—showing him around the New York nightspots, treating him almost as if he were a spoiled son. Many teammates resented it.

But when Werblin departed, Ewbank not only was in complete control, but Namath no longer received special treatment.

So much for the atmosphere in the locker room. The athletes in there also had developed into an important factor.

Ewbank had nurtured his team. Of his best forty players, twenty-four were pure-blooded Jets, meaning those who had never even *attended* another team's training camp. Four others—Jim Turner, Al Atkinson, Winston Hill, and Bill Baird—had been discarded by other clubs as training-camp rookies and thus had never played professionally for another team. Only twelve players, then, had joined the Jets with prior experience in either league.

Of those twelve, Ewbank had kept Don Maynard, Larry Grantham, Bill Mathis, and Curley Johnson from the old Titans. The coach was joined almost immediately in 1963 by two of his former Colts, Bake Turner and Mark Smolinski, and in 1966 by a prodigal son, Johnny Sample, unwanted by the NFL. Only five had experience on other AFL teams—Babe Parilli, Bob Talamini, Billy Joe (now on crutches following knee surgery in November), Paul Rochester, and John Neidert, a reserve linebacker acquired from the Cincinnati Bengals in mid-season.

For casual observers who were under the impression that AFL teams were stocked with NFL rejects, the Jets proved them wrong.

Only five players had competed in the NFL—Parilli and Sample for several years; Maynard, Smolinski, and Bake Turner for brief periods. Essentially, Ewbank had won the AFL championship with *his* players, meaning athletes touted by George Sauer, Sr., the director of player personnel who combed the colleges, and by his assistant coaches, each responsible for a region of colleges. Ewbank's aides also contributed to the players' development, particularly Walt Michaels, the burly architect of the defensive unit, and Clive Rush, the smooth redhead who suggested much of the offensive game plan. Michaels and Rush had been with Ewbank since he reorganized the team in 1963. Two other original aides, Chuck Knox and

J. D. Donaldson, had assisted in the team's eventual ascent, but they had departed and their jobs now were handled by big, friendly Joe Spencer on the offensive line and quiet, scholarly Buddy Ryan on the defensive line.

If Ewbank was blamed when the Jets lost, he deserved most of the credit when they won.

Not that he endeared himself to his players. But in winning the AFL championship, they had begun to understand him. Early in the season, when Namath threw five interceptions in each of two losing games, Ewbank's tolerance annoyed some of them. They believed that he should have benched Namath and inserted Parilli, the old pro.

"I'll use Babe," Ewbank told newsmen, "when I think Babe can do a better job, when he throws better than Joe in practice, when he has better timing than Joe in practice. But as long as Joe is healthy, you go with your number one. Anytime you start taking a quarterback out every time he's intercepted, you're going to ruin him."

His tolerant wisdom worked for Namath, as it had worked when he was developing Johnny Unitas.

"As young quarterbacks, they were very comparable," Ewbank said midway in the 1968 season. "I remember when John was young, people used to ask me to compare him with Otto Graham because I had been with Otto at Cleveland, and I used to say, 'Give John an opportunity to play a few seasons and his record will speak for itself.' It'll be the same way with Joe.

"John had an interception problem, too. The thing about both of them is that they're so good, they thought they could complete anything. I remember I once brought Otto Graham to camp to criticize John in the workouts. One time John completed a pass over the middle and Otto told him, 'You hit that one, but I wouldn't have thrown it into that crowd.'

"Their throwing styles are different. John always followed through with the back of his hand pointed inward, like a baseball pitcher throwing a screwball. I thought he'd have arm trouble sooner. Joe's motion is straight-away. He might avoid having arm trouble. But then Joe has those bad knees that might go on him anytime, so each of them has his problems."

Namath and Unitas are different in temperament—the flashy young swinger and the solid old square.

But again, Ewbank's tolerant wisdom got the best out of what another coach might have botched. During the 1968 season, several Jets let their facial hair grow. Verlon Biggs, the huge defensive end, began to cultivate a goatee. So did Jim Hudson and John Elliott, and several mustaches sprouted. Namath topped them all with his famous Fu Manchu.

Other coaches might have fumed, particularly those with crewcut hair, as Ewbank has. But he seemed to understand.

"As long as they produce," he had said, "I don't care about their beards or mustaches. Their job is to play football."

And they produced so consistently that Wilbur Charles Ewbank of the New York Jets, not Johnny Rauch of the Oakland Raiders or Hank Stram of the Kansas City Chiefs, was about to hold his first Super Bowl meeting as he hobbled on a cane toward the Imperial Room, one of the banquet rooms in the Galt.

"We're going to look at some films of the Colts for the first time," he was saying now. "Nothing special."

Ewbank's plan was to keep his players at a low pitch. The game itself was enough to get them up. His job was to keep them from getting up too high. The practices today, tomorrow, and Sunday would be merely training-camp workouts to establish a "physical tone," as he called it, for the more serious sessions next week.

"We don't want to play 'em right away. We'll take Monday off," he said, "then we'll break a sweat Tuesday after we go over the game plan. We'll concentrate on offense on Wednesday, on defense on Thursday, polish everything on Friday, and taper off on Saturday, just like for any other game."

In the past, the Super Bowl teams had not arrived on the scene until seven days before the game, but Weeb Ewbank wanted his players to be comfortable and relaxed when they began their serious preparation. He wanted them to regain some of their training-camp condition by breaking a sweat in the Florida warmth, an impossibility in the New York chill.

"And I'll be ready for the game," the coach said, tapping his cane and laughing. "I don't have to report my injury to the Commissioner's office until Tuesday."

If necessary, he would go to the game on a stretcher. Through the years, he always hid his resentment of his dismissal by the Colts, but it had torn at him. In his mild manner, he enjoyed a cordial relationship with the members of the Colt organization, but he resented the way he had been fired.

"He's been waiting a long time for a crack at the Colts," one of his confidants would say later, "a long time."

On the day following the 1962 season when he was to meet Carroll Rosenbloom, the Colts' president, Ewbank had been told that he would have the opportunity for a full discussion of the team situation.

"But the *full* discussion," disclosed the confidant, "lasted for about three minutes."

In the Super Bowl game, Wilbur Charles Ewbank would have fifty-seven more minutes to work with.

In their Memorial Stadium locker room, the members of the Baltimore Colts were listening to Don Shula's theme in preparing his players for the Super Bowl game. "Just remember," the coach said, "that everything we've accomplished all season is riding on the outcome of this game."

Before the arrival of Weeb Ewbank, the Jet players had held a private meeting in the Imperial Room. Some had complained about the club policy of making a player pay his wife's Super Bowl expenses. Others griped about a rumor that the club was about to provide watches as symbols of the AFL championship, instead of the treasured rings. Others heard that their AFL title share would be considerably less than the publicized $9,000 estimate.

Later, when the issues were presented to the head coach, he attempted to soothe his players.

Ewbank contended that other Super Bowl teams had made each player pay for his wife's expenses, that no decision had been made yet on the rings, and the AFL office handled the title shares.

"We've got a game to think about," Ewbank concluded, "and let's think about it."

Not all the players were satisfied. Unaccustomed as they were to the possibility of a $15,000 bonanza for winning the Super Bowl, some of them were worrying about a relatively few dollars. In their sudden splash of glory, the Jets had become the *nouveau riche* of sports.

Matt Snell, the fullback, glanced around the room at some of his introverted teammates.

"I wasn't worried about myself, because I blurt things out when they're bothering me," he would say later, "but I was wondering how the quiet guys, like George Sauer and Winston Hill, would take it. I didn't want anything to happen that would affect their concentration on the game."

But once the complaints had been voiced, some players were embarrassed by them. The business at hand was more important. The players were about to see game films of the Colts for the first time. Two large, white screens had been erected at opposite ends of the room. The offensive unit would watch the Colt defense handle the Browns, and the defensive unit would watch the Colt offense operate against the same team. But to dispel the aura of NFL invincibility, Ewbank was about to compare many of the Colts to players on other AFL teams whom the Jets had outplayed.

"Bubba Smith is virtually a rookie, he hardly played a year ago," Ewbank said. "He doesn't have McDole's know-how."

Ron McDole is a defensive end with the Buffalo Bills, a relatively unpublicized performer, but the Jets respect his consistent pass-rushing ability.

"And their Rabbit Smith, Billy Ray Smith, he's like Jim Hunt of the Patriots, and we've been able to handle Hunt."

Ewbank continued with several comparisons to AFL personnel, but he didn't try to minimize John Mackey's talent.

"Their tight end is something super," he acknowledged, "but we can stop him. No tight end can win all by himself."

Soon, in the darkness, the Jets were inspecting the Colts carefully but realistically. Nearly an hour later, when the film reels ended, they looked around at each other in surprise.

"Hell," said Joe Namath when the lights went on, "they're not supermen."

Across the room, assistant coach Walt Michaels addressed the defense.

"We can stop these guys," Michaels said. "I *know* we can stop these guys."

The mental approach had been formed; the complaints had been forgotten.

On the bus to practice, Jim Richards stared out a window, almost in meditation.

Of all the Jets, the 6-foot 1-inch, 180-pound rookie from Virginia Tech was perhaps the quietest. He practiced as a substitute defensive back, but he appeared mostly on the special teams, notably on the kickoff unit where three men next to him—Gary Magner, Lee White, and Billy Joe—had been cut down with knee injuries.

"I can remember Lee's loud groan," he would recall, "but you try to keep it out of your mind."

Despite the casualties, Richards had impressed the coaches with his speed and tackling. Among his teammates on the special units, he would exhort them to prove that they had been underrated, in comparison to the Colts, but whenever he was around the established regulars, he remained silent.

"Rookies," he would say later, "are like little children. They should be seen and not heard."

Joe Namath noticed the white practice jerseys hanging in the lockers of the offensive players. The offensive unit always practices in jerseys of the basic color to be worn in the next game—white or green. The defensive unit would practice here in green jerseys, but the day of the game, the entire team would be wearing white.

"White uniforms," the quarterback touted. "That means we're the good guys."

Weeb Ewbank would be too proud to use his cane at any of the practices. Now in his white baseball cap with a green peak, a green nylon jacket over a white polo shirt, green pants and rubber-soled football shoes, he hopped up the steps of the first-base dugout to inspect the field.

It had been marked out across the outfield grass. Only one set of goalposts had been erected, but one would be enough.

Most important, the grass was green, unlike the brownish grass of Shea Stadium's cement-like surface. The coach was delighted. If any of his players slipped, the grass would protect them. Back at Shea's frozen field, it would be like falling in the street.

Although it was cloudy, it was warm, with the temperature in the mid-seventies. This was important because it made it easier for the players to break a sweat. With the easy drinking some of them were doing at night, Ewbank wanted them to sweat.

As the old coach gazed around the ballpark, he noticed three men in a glass booth atop the grandstand roof behind third base. He had been told about them. Outside the ballpark was the Executive

Airport for private planes. Every so often, a plane would buzz by. The glass booth was the control tower.

When the Packers arrived here for the previous Super Bowl game, Vince Lombardi marched up to identify the occupants of the glass booth. He wanted to assure himself that nobody there was an Oakland Raider spy.

Ewbank was more trusting. Maximum security had been provided. There were no high buildings nearby, where a spy with binoculars might perch undetected and observe the Jets' formations and plays. Nor could a stranger peek through the outfield fence without being caught. Nor would anyone risk climbing the towering royal palm trees.

The only strangers were the members of the stadium ground crew and the uniformed Fort Lauderdale policemen. Weeb Ewbank had to trust somebody.

The workout itself was casual. While the others did calisthenics, Joe Namath and Babe Parilli threw passes to each other, loosening their arms for the offensive drill. The last player to appear was Emerson Boozer, the halfback, who had been detained while trainer Jeff Snedeker taped his surgical knee.

"Hey, Weeb," Namath yelled, "I told you Emerson was going to practice this week."

"It's nice to have you, Emerson," the coach said. "Nice to have you with us here."

They laughed, but later, during the passing drill, one of the most important Jets, flanker Don Maynard, was merely an observer. His left leg was sore. But he promised Ewbank that he would be ready a week from Sunday.

Jim Hudson hadn't been on the charter. He had permission to take his wife Wendy and their small son Treg home to Austin, Texas. But now, after practice, the strong-side safetyman was slumped on the gray wooden bench in front of his locker. He appeared weary.

"Damn airlines," he said.

He's one of those slender Texans blessed with whipcord strength. Tall, dark-haired, and handsome, he's an easy talker, but his narrow-eyed face sometimes has a grouchy look, as if he were a sheriff ordering a troublemaker out of town. Right now, after practice, he was a little grouchier than usual as he explained his problems with the airlines.

"Been on planes two days," he said.

"What happened?" asked a bystander.

"Took my wife and little boy to Newark two days ago to fly to Dallas. We had so much junk, closing out our New York apartment, I had to hire a truck. Missed the plane there, had to wait three hours for the next one. When we got to Dallas, we had to wait four hours for the flight to Austin. By the time we got home, it was three o'clock in the morning. I got a couple hours sleep and got up to come here yesterday. But when I got to Dallas, my flight to Miami had been canceled. Weather or somethin'. Had to wait five hours for one to New Orleans, then I waited another hour in New Orleans to go to Atlanta, and when I got to Atlanta, there were no more flights to Fort Lauderdale. But they had one that stopped in Jacksonville and Tampa going to Miami, so I took it, then jumped a limousine. Got to the hotel at five this morning, five a.m."

"No wonder you look tired."

"And they lost my baggage," he said. "No idea where it is. All I got is the suit I was wearing. Damn airlines."

"Joe's clothes fit you, don't they?"

"Yeah, if I get desperate," he said.

As roommates, Hudson and Namath make an odd couple. They were rookies together—the $427,000 quarterback and the $427 safetyman. Not exactly $427, but none of the pro teams had drafted him. During his senior season at the University of Texas, knee problems had kept him out of several games. But by the time Texas was ready for the Orange Bowl game, he was ready. As the Longhorn quarterback, he collaborated with George Sauer, Jr., on a 69-yard pass play for the winning touchdown. The losing team that New Year's night in 1965 was Alabama. The losing quarterback was Joe Namath.

The next day Namath signed his $427,000 contract. That same day Ewbank contacted Hudson and soon signed him as a free-agent candidate. But at training camp, while impressing the coaches, the 6-foot 2-inch, 210-pound Hudson developed pleurisy. He lost fifteen pounds. He had to be hospitalized for two weeks. Fluid had to be drained from his lungs.

"You won't be strong enough to play for at least six weeks," a doctor told him.

"I'll bet you on that," Hudson replied. "I'll bet you it won't take me that long."

Three weeks later, he appeared in his first AFL game. He has been the strong-side safetyman ever since, one of the defensive unit's leaders, and one of its toughest players. Several months prior to the 1968 season, he had been bitten on the left ankle by a black widow in an Austin restaurant. Such a bite can be fatal, but except for a swollen leg, he survived.

"To show how tough Hud is," tight end Pete Lammons likes to say, "he lived and the spider died."

His temper can flare. During the third quarter of the "Heidi" game in Oakland, he was involved in an inflammable argument with an official over a face mask penalty. He was ejected. As it turned out, the Raiders won that game with a touchdown pass through an area unprotected by Mike D'Amato, his inexperienced replacement. Hudson not only is a dependable pass-defender, but also a sure tackler.

"He's as good a tackler as I've ever seen," says Walt Michaels, the defensive coach. "He's one of the few backs who'll hit you like a linebacker."

His tackling would be tested in his Super Bowl matchup with John Mackey, the big Colt tight end. Around the NFL, it was said that of all those opponents who tackled Mackey, the lucky ones were those who fell off. Several hours earlier, Hudson had seen Mackey on film for the first time.

"What did Mackey make you think about?" a sportswriter asked the safetyman now.

"He made me think," Jim Hudson replied easily, "about doing a good job on him."

On the last bus returning from practice, Joe Namath was reading through a stack of fan mail. Across the aisle, George Sauer, Jr., glanced at the quarterback.

"I've got nothing to read," the split end said. "Let me read some of your mail."

The quarterback didn't even bother to look up. "You're married," he answered.

He was strolling past the pool, toward the lobby, when he heard his name being paged.

"Frank Ramos," the female voice on the loudspeaker said. "Telephone for Frank Ramos."

Ramos is the club's public-relations director. He's not much older than Joe Namath, and he resembles him facially, although on a smaller scale. "Mini-Joe," some of his friends call him. Essentially, his job involves supplying the news media with information and cooperation, but he has many tangential tasks. He also has access to a limited number of game tickets. During the regular season, he is allotted a few complimentary tickets. But at the Super Bowl, with each ticket priced at twelve dollars by Commissioner Pete Rozelle's office, he was responsible for collecting that amount.

When he picked up the phone at the pool bar, an unfamiliar voice greeted him.

"Frank, this is Dr. Phillipson," the voice said. "You remember me—the dentist in Miami the day you got married. You were in my office that morning. I've left several messages for you, Frank, didn't you get any of them?"

"I'm sorry, Doctor, but I thought you were calling Jackie," he said, meaning his wife, Jacqueline.

The morning of their wedding in 1964, they had been in Dr. Phillipson's office to have their teeth cleaned. He hadn't seen him or heard from him since that day, but he realized that the dentist was a friend of his wife's family.

"No, no, I want to talk to you," the dentist was saying now. "Your mother-in-law told me that you had Super Bowl tickets."

"Well, not exactly. I have a few, but they're spoken for, and it doesn't look like I'm going to get any more. I just don't have any that I haven't already promised to people."

"No chance at all?"

"I don't see how."

Disappointed, the dentist thanked him and hung up, but for Frank Ramos, and for all the members of the Jet entourage, the telephone calls for tickets had only begun.

For once, Curley Johnson wasn't laughing or wisecracking. He wasn't even smiling.

"It hurts," the Jet punter was saying after dinner in the Bimini Room. "It hurts like hell."

He was talking about the knee on his kicking leg. In the season's fourth game, he had started at tight end against the San Diego Chargers because Pete Lammons was recuperating from a pulled leg muscle. He caught three passes, an important factor in the 23–20 victory. But on one of them, when he turned to run upfield with the ball, he was tackled hard by safetyman Kenny Graham.

Pain shot through Johnson's right knee. He couldn't run well enough to continue at tight end in the second half. But he did get back into the game to punt.

But what he didn't know was that his kneecap had been cracked for several seasons and when Graham jarred it, a bone chip developed about the size of a quarter. As the pain continued throughout the remainder of the season, he was forced to limit his punting practice. Ordinarily, he punted about thirty times each Wednesday and Friday, but he had to stop now after about ten because of the severe swelling behind his knee.

Not that it limited his sense of humor, the sharpest on the team, as all the players had known for some time.

"This is your pilot speaking," a voice once crackled over the intercom on a Jets' charter flight. "We are at 2,000 feet and preparing to land. If you will look out of the windows to the right, you will see a man floating to earth in a parachute. This is a recording."

The players laughed. Even the pilot laughed. John Curley Johnson, whose brown hair isn't curly, had struck again.

Another time, when the Jets were training at the Peekskill Military Academy outside of New York City during Joe Namath's rookie year, the quarterback received a phone call from a soft-voiced female who offered to meet him downtown. Namath arrived at the appointed time, but after waiting twenty minutes, no girl showed up. Suddenly, he noticed a group of teammates strolling toward him.

"Hello, dahlin'," Curley called.

Namath knew he had been tricked.

At the age of 33, the thick-set 6-foot, 215-pound punter was the second oldest on the team. Out of the University of Houston, he was a rookie with the Colts in 1958, but he spent the season on Weeb Ewbank's taxi squad. The following year, he played for the Montreal Alouettes of the Canadian Football League. He joined the Dallas Texans (now the Kansas City Chiefs) in 1960 when the AFL began. He was traded to the Titans during the 1962 season. In addition to punting, he occasionally was employed as a running back and a tight end, adding to his usefulness.

"You know what I'd like to be?" he once said. "I'd like to be a great runner. I just didn't have the speed."

At least not with his feet. But with a wisecrack, no one was faster. But there was nothing funny about his knee. Several weeks after the game, the knee would require bone-chip surgery, but now, as he painfully flexed his knee after dinner, he thought he had incurred cartilage damage.

"And as long as I can punt," he was saying now without a smile, "I won't let anybody cut on me."

Out over the ocean, National Airlines flight 91 from New York was on its glide path to Miami International Airport.

In seat 3A of the first-class section was an unusual passenger—a large brown cardboard box. Inside it, packed in cotton, was the sterling silver Super Bowl trophy—a football atop a curved triangular base with the AFL and NFL emblems above an inscription, "World Professional Football Championship." In the next seat was Chris Vecsey, an aide in Commissioner Rozelle's office in New York City.

With a chartered limousine at his disposal in New York, Vecsey had picked up the packaged trophy at Tiffany's and had been driven to LaGuardia Airport. There he checked in at the gate with two first-class tickets, one for himself, one for the trophy.

"But all the way down," Vecsey would say later when the trophy was locked safely at Super Bowl headquarters in the Hilton Plaza Hotel in Miami Beach, "I kept worrying that the plane would be hijacked to Cuba and that Castro's soldiers would impound it and Castro would have it melted down like Cromwell did in England when he melted all the gold and silver and turned them into coins. And there'd be no trophy."

In the Howard Johnson's across the street, Don Maynard was ordering a late snack.

"I'll have a grilled-cheese sandwich with a slice of ham in it, please," he said in his Texas twang, "and a chocolate Coke."

"That's a *chocolate* Coke, sir?" the counter-girl asked. "*Chocolate* syrup in it?"

"Yes, ma'am, the chocolate kills the strongness of the Coke a little. You ought to try it yourself."

"No, thank you," she said.

Don Maynard of the Jets is a fragile individualist. He's slender, almost skinny at 6-foot 1-inch tall and 180 pounds. His ropy muscles are 31 years old, a dangerous age because he depends on speed, as a flanker must. One of those muscles, the hamstring in his left thigh, had been frayed nearly four weeks earlier as he ran a go pattern in the next-to-last game of the regular season. He had performed spectacularly in the AFL championship game catching two touchdown passes, but he had aggravated the muscle pull.

"It's there," he said now, sipping his chocolate Coke, "but I'll be there a week from Sunday. I waited a long time."

He had waited in frustration. But typically, he was an individualist throughout. When he joined the New York Giants in 1958 as a rookie out of what is now known as the University of Texas at El Paso, he arrived as a Texan should—wearing cowboy boots, blue jeans, and sideburns. This was a decade before sideburns were stylish. Instead of realizing that Maynard was ten years ahead of his time, several Giant officials suggested that he shave them off. "No, sir," said Don Maynard.

When he reported to training camp the following summer, he displeased Allie Sherman, then a new assistant coach, with his long strides in running a pass pattern.

"This isn't a track meet," Sherman said. "Shorten your strides."

"I cover more ground in one stride," said the individualist, "than anybody else around here does in three."

The day of the next cut, the Giants released Maynard.

Packing his boots and his blue jeans, he signed with the Hamilton

Tiger-Cats of the Canadian Football League. But when the AFL began operations in 1960, he returned to New York with the Titans. Installed at flanker by Sammy Baugh, who knew Maynard's reputation when he coached at Hardin-Simmons in Texas, he started to accumulate yardage as a pass-receiver—1,265 that first year.

Yard by yard, it began to add up. But his accomplishments were clouded by the AFL's reputation for poor pass-defense.

During the early seasons of the AFL, he did outmaneuver many unskilled cornerbacks, although his own quarterback was often unskilled, too. He also was accumulating yardage as an El Paso businessman. He developed a butane business, a cleaning business, a golf-cart business, a credit-card business, and he also taught mathematics and industrial arts in a high school.

But his main business was catching passes. When Joe Namath joined the Jets in 1965, business boomed.

In four seasons with Namath as the starting quarterback, he caught 244 passes for 4,789 yards and 39 touchdowns—remarkable statistics. Not that he stopped being an individualist. On the field, he occasionally altered his pass-pattern, signaling the quarterback with a raised arm. If the quarterback saw him, Maynard's move sometimes resulted in a touchdown. If the quarterback missed it, the move sometimes resulted in an interception. Off the field, he also altered the patterns occasionally, such as the early December night in Oakland in 1966 when the water shone in the Edgewater Inn's outdoor swimming pool.

'That water's so pretty," one of the Jets suggested after dinner, "that somebody ought to dive in."

"Put up some money," said the individualist, "and I'll do it. But you've got to make it worthwhile."

"No bathing suit," another player said. "Just like you are. With your clothes on. And off the board."

Maynard agreed. He was permitted to take off his black cowboy boots and black socks. Tiptoeing out to the end of the 8-foot board in his black slacks, shirt, tie, and green Jet blazer, he glanced at Mike Taliaferro, then the second-string quarterback.

"How much money you got there for me?" he asked.

"Fifty-seven dollars," Taliaferro said. "That enough?"

"That's enough," Maynard answered.

Soaring gracefully in a full gainer, he splashed into the chilled water. Surfacing, he easily stroked the length of the 25-yard pool, to the shouts and cheers of his teammates. When he emerged, his clothes dripping, he stuffed the fifty-seven dollars into one of his wet pockets, grabbed his boots and socks, and ran to his room, to the accompaniment of more cheers. When he had disappeared, a teammate smiled.

"Put up enough money," he said, "and ol' Maynard would swim the Atlantic."

Maynard had established a reputation among his teammates for watching his pennies. As a sales representative of Swipe, a cleaning fluid, he sold the item to his teammates for three dollars and two cents. "And you better believe," says Weeb Ewbank, "that he gets the two cents." He makes AFL cornerbacks pay, too. Near the end of the 1968 season, he established a career record for pass-reception yardage by a pro, surpassing the 9,275 yards accumulated by Raymond Berry of the Baltimore Colts, one of Johnny Unitas's favorite targets prior to his retirement following the 1967 season.

By the end of the season, Maynard's career total was more than five miles long, 9,435 yards on 504 receptions, 78 for touchdowns. Included were 84 yards on five receptions in that one season with the Giants when he was remembered mostly for his sideburns and for fumbling a punt in the Eastern Conference playoff game with the Cleveland Browns, which the Giants won, 10–0. But ever since, Giant fans had snickered at him because he hadn't made it in the NFL, and those snickers had annoyed the individualist for ten years as he waited for a chance for vindication.

Now, as he finished his sandwich in Howard Johnson's, he held *the* record for pass-reception yardage.

"And that record," he was saying, "is why I want to play a couple more years. I want to keep adding yardage so I'll have that record a little while longer."

Not far behind was Lance Alworth of the San Diego Chargers, and an eventual challenger would be Maynard's teammate, George Sauer, Jr.

"That record is nice to have for the prestige," said the man with a reputation of counting every penny. "It's like this Super Bowl game. The money's nice, but you spend the money. It's the prestige that counts. The prestige."

SATURDAY, JANUARY 4
"It's Time I Tapped That Knee"

The weather hadn't changed. Dark gray clouds swept across the sky above the Galt and out over the ocean. But in the Bimini Room at breakfast, Paul "Rocky" Rochester's face glowed. When the waitress passed out the menus, he winked at his brother Phil.

"Chow down," the defensive tackle said. "We got somebody else paying for this, an expense-account man."

Rocky laughed. So did his 17-year-old brother. And so did a sportswriter with an expense account. Rocky Rochester laughs often, but he was *happier* than usual. His brother's presence was responsible for that. He hadn't known where his brother was for several weeks following a phone call to their uncle, Art Rochester, in Grand Rapids, Michigan, where Rocky assumed Phil was living. "I told Art," Rocky was saying, "that I wanted Phil to come to New York for the championship game, and he told me that he didn't know where Phil was, that he ran away two months before with the clothes on his back.

"I asked him if he'd called the police, and he said that he had, but that they couldn't do much unless Phil got into trouble and nothing like that had happened. I knew they hadn't seen eye-to-eye, but I wanted to know why he hadn't told me about it when it happened, and he said that he didn't want to worry me with the season on, and that he kept thinking that Phil would be back any day.

43

"But that wasn't doing me any good," Rocky said, his hoarse voice unusually serious. "I had to find him."

The brothers and their sister, Diane, had been orphaned in 1955. Their 46-year-old father had died suddenly of a heart attack. Soon their 41-year-old mother also died.

"She just kind of gave up," Rocky continued, "and Phil and I were 13 years apart. That was a problem."

Rocky was invited to live with Marc Martone, his football coach at Sewanhaka High School in Floral Park, New York, not too far from Shea Stadium, while Phil, then 4, joined his uncle in Grand Rapids. To be nearer to him, Rocky later chose Michigan State of all the colleges that had offered him a football scholarship. But when he entered the AFL in 1960, he was separated from his brother for months at a time. In addition, he had his own problems to worry about.

During the 1963 season, he was waived to the Jets by the Kansas City Chiefs when their coach, Hank Stram, believed that the AFL had "outgrown" a player of Rochester's unspectacular skills.

Although not as big as some defensive tackles, and not as quick as others, the 6-foot 2-inch, 250-pound Rochester established himself as one of the Jets' most reliable linemen. But in a 1966 game in Oakland, a teammate, Verlon Biggs, accidentally stuck a finger into Rochester's left eye during a pileup. Momentarily blinded in that eye, he groped his way to the sideline. But he later returned to the game and blocked a field goal in the 28–28 tie.

When he awoke the next morning, the eye was clouded with blood. Jeff Snedeker, the trainer, ordered him to a hospital.

"There are three layers in an eye, like an onion," Rocky says with authority, "and the middle layer had ruptured and hemorrhaged. At first the doctors thought they would have to remove the eye, but I was lucky. For two weeks I couldn't move, but when they took the bandages off, I was all right. I mean my sight had gone to 20/200, but I was all right"

Not completely. His pupil is dilated constantly, and on a sunny day, he gets a headache easily.

"I don't use a contact lens in it," he says. "I rely on experience. When you've been around as long as I have, you can smell the play. You know where the guard is, and you know where the quarterback is."

But for several weeks, he hadn't known where his brother Phil was. Naturally, it disturbed him.

"I'd see him in the summer," he was saying now, "but we lost each other for a lot of years."

The day of the AFL championship game, he explained the situation to two National Broadcasting Company announcers, Curt Gowdy and Charlie Jones, and they agreed to mention that Phil should contact his older brother.

"I knew that no matter where Phil was," Rocky said, "that he would have the game on."

"I was painting my apartment when I heard it," Phil said.

He was sharing an apartment in Grand Rapids with a buddy, Jim Falstrom, while working in a gas station.

"And three minutes after the game," he continued, "we got in my blue Chevy . . ."

"Blue and rust," Rocky interrupted, his hoarse laugh booming, "a rusty old '55."

"Three minutes after the game," Phil repeated, smiling below his thin mustache, "we were on the way. We didn't have enough money. I had fifteen dollars, and he had five, and when we got down into Indiana, we panhandled in a restaurant. But we kept going, and we stopped at our sister's place in Paoli, Pennsylvania. After we left there, she called Paul and told him that we were on our way to his home in Port Washington, out on Long Island. But we got lost in Brooklyn before we finally got there New Year's Eve."

The day before, Phil accompanied Rocky on the charter. He would be with him throughout the stay at the Galt.

"He's going to finish high school," Rocky was saying now. "He quit school to work in a gas station, but he only needs two semesters and then he's going to college. Some of my Super Bowl money will take care of that, but right now we're enjoying being with each other. We lost each other for a lot of years."

Mixing among the players was the Jets' orthopedic specialist, Dr. James A. Nicholas, husky, dark-haired, 47 years old, with horned-rim glasses and a compulsive smile. He had been around the team since 1960 when he volunteered to look after the players following the death of a Titan guard, Howard Glenn, who broke his neck in a game at Houston.

In that time, he had performed a total of sixty-one knee operations on forty-eight different players.

His most famous football patient was Joe Namath, of course, but he had aided in the fourth spinal surgery on John F. Kennedy, and he had operated on Greta Garbo, Claudette Colbert, Angela Lansbury, and Peter Lawford.

He had taken a week off from his busy office on East 77th Street in New York City to supervise the medical preparations for the Jets.

Ordinarily, when John Schmitt shakes hands with somebody, the other person feels it. The center is 6-feet 4-inches tall and 245 pounds, with the huge hands that he needs to snap the football. But as he shook hands in the lobby with a much smaller, much weaker friend, he winced and pulled his right paw away, then held it tenderly.

"What's the matter?" the friend asked.

"I hurt it in the championship game," Schmitt said. "I was moving back to pass-block, and when I looked for the linebacker, I turned. My hand was out, and just as I turned, it got caught between Talamini and Oats, between their chests."

Bob Talamini, the Jets' left guard, is 255 pounds, and Carleton Oats of the Raiders is 260 pounds.

"It was like getting it caught in a door," he said. "But it'll be okay, it has to be okay."

John Schmitt would need a healthy hand to snap the ball properly to Joe Namath and to Babe Parilli, who spots the ball for place-kicker Jim Turner. It's an unlikely profession for a 26-year-old insurance agent who had been a two-way tackle at Hofstra University and who was ignored by all the professional teams in the player draft.

"But my coach, Howdy Myers, suggested that the Jets look at me," he has said. "I remember George Sauer, Sr., came out and gave me a ball and told me to keep it and learn to snap it."

After the Jets signed him as a free agent, he qualified for the forty-man roster in 1964, but he didn't play much. Mike Hudock was the center. But late in the 1965 season, he emerged as the regular, and Hudock went to the Miami Dolphins in the expansion draft. Since then, John Schmitt has started every game as the center.

"In 1966," he likes to say, "they had eight centers in camp, but I was the only one that stayed."

Except for the nuance of where to position the laces on the ball, his task is brutally basic: block.

"On a regular play, the laces should be up, so they come into Joe's hand ready for him to grip it for a pass," he once explained. "On a place-kick, they should be on the bottom, because we've worked it out that at seven yards, the ball will take enough revolutions so that when Babe gets it, the laces are facing the goalposts, not Jim's foot. But on the offensive line, we like to say that we're in 'The Silent Service.' The only time you hear your name is when you miss a block."

John Schmitt doesn't miss many.

"On a regular play, at least I can see the guy I'm supposed to block because my head is up. I only have to lift the ball into the quarterback's hands. But on a place-kick, my head is down, and I'm looking upside down at Babe's hands. When I snap the ball, I know that I'm going to get blasted. On a place-kick, the other team always puts their biggest man right on my nose to blast me. That's why a lineman's biggest satisfaction is in blasting his man back, really knocking his block off."

To the spectators, the center, perhaps more than any other lineman, usually is unseen and unappreciated.

"My reward," he has said, "is having Joe say, 'You gave me a lot of time on that pass,' or having one of the backs come back and slap me on the fanny."

But for the opportunity of receiving that reward in the Super Bowl game, he would need a healthy hand.

"Jeff," he was saying now to trainer Snedeker in the lobby, "remind me to put on an Ace bandage after practice so that I won't have to shake hands with people. All morning I've been shaking hands with people. My hand will never get better that way."

The coaches were up early, and since nine o'clock, they had been in the Directors Room, a small conference room in the far wing of the Galt. They were busy viewing the Colt films in order to assemble the game plan. As the defensive coach, Walt Michaels had to type Earl Morrall's choice of plays in various situations.

"Morrall likes to go to Mackey on third down," Michaels was saying now.

"I don't blame him," Weeb Ewbank said. "Mackey is really something super."

At the other end of the room, Clive Rush and Joe Spencer were looking over the Colt defense, and Ewbank would wander between the two screens.

"They show the safety blitz a lot," Rush mentioned.

"Let them come with it," Ewbank said. "We haven't missed picking up a safety blitz all year, and Joe can get the ball away before they get to him anyway."

"Nobody," said Spencer, the offensive line coach, "is going to get to him."

At the noon meeting, the players again viewed Colt films. When they were through, Curley Johnson shook his head.

"If their defense doesn't do any more than that," he said, "Joe will get us points. I just know Joe will get us in."

But at the moment, the quarterback's passing thumb was bothering him, as it had bothered him throughout much of the season. He has what Dr. Nicholas calls an "unstable thumb," meaning it's double-jointed and it gets whacked out of position from time to time. During the meeting, the quarterback wore a hot pack on his thumb, with a plastic bag around his hand to keep the heat in. But when he arrived at Fort Lauderdale Stadium, he discarded the hot pack and put on his red jersey and gray sweat pants. In practice, the Jet quarterbacks wear red jerseys to remind their teammates to avoid crashing into them. Outside, the sun broke through the clouds and flashed through the high windows of Ewbank's locker-room office.

"Look at that," the coach said. "The Man Upstairs must be on our side."

The casual workout began with calisthenics—jumping-jacks, toe-touching, side twists, situps, pushups, and leg raises. But now, as most of the players left the field after the workout, Joe Spencer, the 6-foot 4-inch, 260-pound coach who wears a size-50 extra-long jacket, was about to put both the offensive and defensive linemen through the grass drill.

"Get over here, or go home," Spencer barked. "Do we have a choice?" asked Rocky Rochester. Torturous is the word for the grass drill, one of the most severe conditioning exercises in football. "Down," snapped Spencer.

And a dozen huge men, flopping like so many beached porpoises, fell forward onto their chests and rolled slightly to one side.

"Up," yelled their drill-master. "Back."

Down they sat. Up again. Down to the right. Up. Down to the left. Up. Over and over again. After about thirty-five of these four-part sequences, Spencer halted them for a brief rest, then he put them through about thirty more. When they finished, the sweat was dripping off their noses and chins and ears, as if they were leaky faucets. Minutes later, Larry Grantham yanked his rubber shirt over his head and the sweat puddled the cement floor of the locker room.

"If you dance to the tune," said Grantham, who had a few beers the night before, "you got to pay the fiddler."

Looking into the mirror on one of the locker-room pillars, Winston Hill was brushing his hair when a sportswriter approached.

"Winnie," the sportswriter asked, "what do you remember about the time you were in training camp with the Colts back in 1963?"

"Nothing," said the 6-foot 4-inch, 280-pound offensive left tackle. "Every few years I go back over my life and cross out everything that's unpleasant."

Behind him, George Sauer, Jr., leaned his chin on Hill's wide left shoulder.

"Then," Sauer said, "why don't you cross out your face?"

Hill smiled. He doesn't smile often, especially these days. Out of Texas Southern, he had been drafted by the Colts when Ewbank was still the coach. But by the time he reported to training camp, Ewbank had been dismissed. During the early workouts, Hill presumed that he was impressing the coaches. One day he was instructed to report to Don Shula's office. He assumed that Shula was going to tell him how well he was doing.

"Winston," the coach began. "I'm sorry, but we're going to have to let you go."

Shula went on to explain that Bob Vogel, an offensive tackle from Ohio State who had been their number-one draft choice, was about to join the squad. As a member of the College All-Star team, Vogel had been detained. Hill, meanwhile, had failed to handle Ordell Braase, the Colts' experienced defensive end.

"We're only going to keep one rookie offensive tackle," Shula said, "but if you're interested in the AFL, try the Jets."

Shula mentioned that he had alerted Ewbank to Hill's potential, but the gigantic rookie already had another idea.

"I had been told by the Denver Broncos," he once said, "that if Baltimore cut me, to call them, so I did. Collect. But they wouldn't accept the call. So then I called Weeb, and he told me to come up to the Jets' camp. After a few days there, he told me he couldn't use me. I told him I wasn't leaving. He just looked at me, so I told him again. I told him I knew I could make his team, even if I had to stay in New York at my own expense. My grandfather, my great-uncle, and my father played college ball when everybody said they couldn't make it, and I wasn't ready to accept that I had found something I couldn't conquer."

Ewbank doesn't remember that confrontation. But Hill does, in detail.

"He told me that I could stay on at the Jets' expense if I'd try to learn a second position—center. I centered that ball until I couldn't see, and I bugged Sherman Plunkett about how to play tackle."

Plunkett, whose weight fluctuated around the 300-pound mark, was a tremendous pass-blocker. Hill was a tremendous student. When the 1963 Jet team was announced, the resourceful rookie was on the squad.

"That first season," Hill said, "I was mostly on the special teams. But in 1964, I was a regular."

He has been ever since. As a high-school athlete, he had been a standout tennis player. The agility necessary for tennis, plus his size and strength, resulted in his development into one of the AFL's best offensive tackles. But inside his head, as he brushed his hair now in front of the mirror in the locker room, was the haunting memory of that Colt training camp when Ordell Braase, whom he would have to block a week from tomorrow, had continually fooled him.

"I don't remember anything about it," he repeated. "Nothing at all."

He meant that he didn't *want* to remember how Ordell Braase had made him look bad.

Near his locker, Joe Namath was putting on a pair of brown plaid bermuda shorts. Murray Janoff of the *Long Island Press* had a Miami newspaper folded under his arm, and Namath nodded at a headline about a meeting the baseball owners had scheduled to select a new Commissioner.

"When's the meeting?" the quarterback asked.

"In a few weeks," Janoff said. "Why, do you want the job?"

"No chance. You got to have short hair. No sideburns."

Gerry Philbin was strolling toward the Galt's shopping arcade when he noticed John Stofa, a college teammate.

In his competitive credo, Philbin once referred to Stofa, a quarterback for the Cincinnati Bengals, as "the only friend" he had on the other AFL teams. They had played together at the University of Buffalo before Philbin developed into an All-AFL defensive end and Stofa emerged as a quarterback for the Miami Dolphins, prior to being traded to the Bengals. In the lobby now, after greeting each other, Stofa nodded toward his companion, another quarterback, Rick Norton of the Dolphins.

"You've met Rick, haven't you?" Stofa asked.

"Only on the field," Philbin said. "We've never had a formal introduction."

As they shook hands, Philbin noticed a bloodied scab near Norton's left ear.

"What happened?" Philbin asked.

"I forgot to duck," Norton said. "My jaw was broken."

"When?"

"Our last game of the season, when you were here."

"How'd it happen?"

"You whacked me in the face," Norton said, smirking.

"*Me?*"

"You!"

"I don't even remember it," Philbin said. "I'm sorry, I didn't mean to hurt you."

"Forget it," Norton said. "It's part of the game."

It's a big part of Gerry Philbin's game. Personally, he was sorry that he had injured Norton. Professionally, that had been his objective. At a sturdy 245 pounds and with shoulders so big that they appear constantly hunched, he is not among the AFL's biggest defensive ends. But he might be the quickest. He surely is one of the most dedicated. Mostly he is dedicated to flattening quarterbacks.

"I don't hate anybody out there," he has said, "but this is a game of hitting. You're trying to hit them, not dirty, but hit them hard and make them feel it. And if you can put a quarterback out of the game, it makes it easier for your team to win."

His philosophy had been formed as a schoolboy in Pawtucket, Rhode Island. He developed it further at the University of Buffalo, where he was coached by Buddy Ryan (the current Jet aide) and where he was spotted by George Sauer, Sr., the Jets' director of player personnel. Sauer attended a Buffalo-Delaware game to scout Stofa on a cold, cloudy afternoon in 1963. When it began to rain, he turned to his wife Lillian.

"Why don't you wait in the car?" he suggested. "There's no need for you to get drenched, too."

As the game progressed, Sauer was distracted by Philbin's aggressive performance. But by the time lie rejoined his wife, he was wet and shivering.

"I thought you'd be here sooner," she said.

"I saw a good football player," he explained.

"No player is worth pneumonia."

"This one is," George Sauer said, smiling.

Not long after that, the Jets selected Philbin in the college draft, much to his surprise. In the days prior to draft, he had been contacted by the Green Bay Packers, the Los Angeles Rams, and the

Detroit Lions, but it wasn't until the night before the draft that a Jet representative phoned.

"I've forgotten whether it was Weeb or Walt Michaels," he said, "but he asked me if I'd be interested in playing in New York. I told him sure."

Philbin also was drafted by the Lions, but the Jets outbid them. After being hindered as a rookie by a shoulder separation, he soon developed into one of the AFL's most feared players. In repose, he is pleasant, calm, almost detached. But when he puts on his Jet uniform, he is transformed. Once, after a game with the Denver Broncos, he was talking about how he had smashed quarterback Steve Tensi.

"I thought I had him, I thought I got his knee," he said. "I had a 10-yard run at him. I really thought I had him."

Tensi survived. Philbin does not look fondly on running backs, either. When the Jets opposed the Bengals late in the 1968 season, halfback Paul Robinson had already accumulated 990 yards as a runner in his rookie year. It would be his final game, and with the Jets having clinched the Eastern Division title, certainly it seemed the Jets would not have to make him their special concern. There was no reason to doubt that he would surpass the 1,000-yard mark. No reason except that Gerry Philbin was exhorting his teammates on the defensive unit to prevent Robinson from gaining a net total of more than nine yards.

"If we can keep him under 1,000," Philbin said, "that'll be something for him to remember."

The Jet defensive unit almost succeeded. Robinson would gain 3 yards, then lose 7, gain 12, then lose 8. But he finished the game with a net total of 33 yards, enough to assure his 1,000-yard accomplishment.

"Damn it, we almost did it," Philbin complained later without a smile.

Another one of Philbin's commandments is not to smile during a football game.

"I despise guys who are friendly, who joke around," he once said. "You're out there to kick hell out of the other guy or get hell kicked out of you. If you smile and joke, the next time you may not hit him as hard as you could, and that makes it easier on him. There have been guys on this team who have done that. It gets me upset."

With his unrelenting determination to excel, perhaps it's just as well that he's somewhat undersized for a defensive end.

"If I was as big as Verlon Biggs," he once said about his 270-pound teammate, "I'd make people pay me to let them live."

But now, as he stood in the lobby of the Galt with John Stofa and Rick Norton, he again apologized for the broken jaw.

"Don't worry about it," Norton said, "but if you get a good shot at Earl Morrall, just hit him as hard as you hit me."

Like everyone else, the doctor, Jim Nicholas, was there to work. He was about to examine his most famous football patient in the Governor's Suite, but for once, Joe Namath was not primarily concerned with his knee ailments.

"Will you check my arm?" the quarterback asked.

His right arm is his great gift, but ten days earlier, during the Thursday practice before the championship game with the Raiders, pain had seared his triceps muscle—a long, thick muscle from the back of the shoulder to the back of the elbow. It alarmed him because throughout all his years of throwing passes, his arm had never hurt.

"Has it bothered you here?" the doctor said.

"No, and it hasn't bothered me since that day. It was all right in the championship game, but I just want you to check it."

Probing with his fingers, the doctor discovered several small tight spots and massaged them.

"It doesn't seem serious," the doctor said. "But be careful. If it hurts, stop throwing. If it hurts the least bit, tell me immediately."

"Don't worry, I will."

"All right," the doctor said. "Sit over on the couch and put your leg up on the cocktail table. It's about time that I tapped that knee."

"Here we go again," the quarterback said.

He automatically lifted his right leg, the one with the bloated knee, the one with the two curving surgical scars. It had been injured during his final season at Alabama. On a roll-out play, he was running to his right when he stopped to change direction. His knee collapsed. But he didn't undergo surgery until after he signed his contract with the Jets three months later. In that time, the anterior cruciate ligament, which resembles a big rubber band, had disintegrated. Its resiliency had disappeared. In that first operation, Dr. Nicholas was unable to repair that ligament, but he tightened the inside ligament, removed the medial cartilage, which does the work of shock-absorber, and also removed a cyst in the back of the knee joint.

Two years later, shortly after Christmas in 1966, another operation resulted in the removal of the lateral cartilage, the rerouting of two tendons in the back of the knee, and the removal of twenty-two fragments of bone.

His left knee also ached him constantly. Nine months before the Jets' victory in the AFL championship game, he needed surgery to eliminate pain from an inflamed tendon in the left knee. The operation involved the repair of a torn tendon, repair of a ligament, and the removal of cartilage. But after two weeks at training camp, the pain returned. The 6-foot 2-inch Namath throws a pass with the weight of his 195 pounds on his left leg, aggravating the tendon. And in backpedaling to pass, he has a unique tiptoe style that puts extra pressure on his knees. That pressure contributes to the inflammation of the tendon at the base of his left kneecap and to the formation of fluid in his battered right knee.

Such fluid is known as water on the knee. To lessen the pain, that fluid must be drained.

"Aspirated" is the medical term for draining. His right knee had required it twice early in the season and now, with his leg resting on a folded white bath towel on a cocktail table in the Governor's Suite, it was about to be aspirated again.

"There it is," Namath moaned.

The needle was 3 inches long and 1/16 of an inch in diameter, quite thick for a needle. Jeff Snedeker had swabbed the outside of the knee with an antiseptic and with Novocaine. With the needle screwed onto a black-trimmed plastic syringe, Dr. Nicholas slowly inserted it above the outside of the kneecap.

"Daaammmnnn!" the quarterback said.

"You always like to let me know how much you're suffering, don't you?" the doctor said, smiling.

"If I don't, who will?"

Not far away, Jim Hudson, the quarterback's roommate, had been watching, but now he turned away.

"Doc," said Hudson, "you're a sadist."

The doctor smiled, but he was not distracted from his task. With about two inches of the needle inserted, he began to squeeze above and around the swollen knee. Suddenly fluid the color of beer appeared in the syringe. As the doctor continued to squeeze, the flow increased. After about thirty seconds, no more appeared, and he withdrew the needle.

"Very good," the doctor said. "About two ounces."

"I'm lighter," Namath joked. "I'm a scrambler."

The doctor smiled, swabbed the knee with an antiseptic again, and placed a small bandage on the spot, now slightly bloodied, where the needle had entered.

"Try to stay off it tonight," the doctor said.

"I have to go out," the quarterback said. "I'm having dinner at Mr. Werblin's."

"You know what you should do," the doctor said.

The doctor was finished treating the quarterback, but Don Maynard and Al Atkinson, the thick-chested middle linebacker, were waiting to be examined in Snedeker's room. When the doctor arrived, they were watching television.

"How's it feel?" the doctor asked Maynard about his left thigh.

"It's all right walkin', but I'm afraid to run on it," the flanker said. "I feel it if I jog."

"Let me feel it," the doctor said, probing with his fingers.

"Keep pushing around until you hit it," Maynard said.

"You're amazing," the doctor said. "You can recognize a sore spot the size of a pinhead."

"That's it!" Maynard yipped. "You got it, Doc."

"All right," the doctor said, "I'll give you some Cortisone, and whenever you're in your room, keep hot packs on it."

Hopefully, an injection of Cortril, a milky-white liquid, would ease Maynard's injury. The doctor turned to Atkinson.

"You need Cortisone, too, and stay off that leg."

The middle linebacker had stretched several calf muscles in his left leg on Sunday during the AFL championship game.

"Stay off that leg for a few days," the doctor ordered.

"But I've got to practice, Doc," said Atkinson, anxiously.

"Stay off it the next few days, or you might not be able to play next week, I'm serious. What you have can lead to a ruptured Achilles tendon. I'm very serious. Stay off that leg the next few days or you might not be able to play."

The middle linebacker was shocked by the doctor's prognosis. He had no idea his injury was that serious.

When the narrow ramp clanked down out of the rear of the Colts' chartered plane, about 250 people swarmed onto the cement apron of Fort Lauderdale International Airport to greet the NFL champions. One by one, the players filed down the aluminum steps and headed toward two nearby buses as people waved autograph books and ballpoint pens at them. Suddenly, a tall, crew-cut man with a soft, almost sad expression appeared.

"Earl, hey, Earl," some people shouted. "Way to go, Earl. Beat the Jets, Earl."

Earl Morrall, the quarterback whom the New York Giants deemed expendable in August, had guided the Colts to a 13–1 won-lost record during the regular season (losing only to the Browns, 30–20), to a 24–14 victory over the Minnesota Vikings for the Western Conference title, and to a 34–0 rout of the Browns in the championship game. After twelve seasons of relative obscurity with four other NFL teams, he had emerged as a star.

And while Morrall was surrounded as he made his way to the buses, other Colts followed him. Among them was Johnny Unitas, once the king of the quarterbacks but now merely a sore-armed substitute. In his shirt sleeves, unnoticed by the small boys, he boarded one of the buses without being asked for an autograph.

Off to one side, in a dazzle of television lights, Coach Don Shula answered several questions easily. Yes, it had been cold in Baltimore, the ground had been frozen, in fact, but his team had practiced well. No, his practices at St. Andrew's School in nearby Boca Raton would not be open to the public because the Jets could have a spy stationed among the spectators. When the interview ended, Bill Johns of the Statler Hilton Hotel, where the Colts were staying, approached the coach.

"Don," he said, "I've got a limousine to take you to the hotel."

"No, thank you," the coach said. "I always ride with my players."

Outside, the surf tumbled up the sand in front of Sonny Werblin's home in Golden Beach, about half an hour's drive down Route A1A from the Galt. The former president of the Jets was drinking Bell's 12 scotch on the rocks, and he was talking with Dick Young, a sports columnist for the New York *Daily News*.

"The price is ridiculous," Werblin was saying. "It's up to 18 now."

Enough money had been bet on the Colts to add a point to the spread.

"What's so great about Baltimore's running game?" Werblin continued. "They say the Jets have no running game. It's as good as Baltimore's, even better. What's so great about Matte and Hill? Snell and Boozer are as good as they are, even better. The Jets would have won the division title last year if Snell and Boozer hadn't been injured. Maybe I'll be wrong, but they're still my boys, and I want them to win. It's the same team. It would be different if they had changed a lot of players, but they're still my boys."

Of all the Jets, his boy is Joe Namath, the one he signed in 1965 to the contract that changed the AFL's image.

"In all my career," he went on, "I've never met a man whose word meant more than Joe Namath's. I can remember when we were trying to sign him. I called Bear Bryant about it. He asked me if I had Joe's word, and I told him I had, but that I'd like to have something on paper. Bear said that I didn't need it, that if Joe gave me his word, I didn't need anything on paper."

Among the dinner guests at the Werblins' that night would be Namath and Jim Hudson.

"And that's one reason I think the Jets will win. Hudson can handle John Mackey because Hudson is bigger than most strong-side safetymen. He's fast, he's strong, and he hits hard. Pete Rozelle once told me that he had reports that Hudson takes pills, but I told him that it wasn't so, that if Hudson took pills, he'd be in orbit. He's just one of those wild-eyed Texans, he and Pete Lammons. I've always said that if I'm in a fight, I'd want Hudson and Lammons on my side. They're the kind that smile while they kill you."

And the more he talked about his boys, the more he was sure that the 18-point betting line was ridiculous.

"I haven't bet on a football game in eight years," Sonny Werblin said, "but I have to go for this price."

At the Statler Hilton, the Colts had checked into their rooms and now some of them were drifting through the lobby and the Don

Quixote dining room. One of the drifters was Lou Michaels, their place-kicker and the younger brother of Walt Michaels, the Jets' defensive coach.

"Did you call Walt yet?" somebody asked him.

"I'm not even going to talk to him until after the game, if he still wants to talk then."

"You're not going to talk to your brother?"

"And he won't be talking to me, you watch."

They understood each other perfectly. Until the Super Bowl game was over, they were rivals, and to them, that was thicker than blood. It was part of their upbringing in the Eastern Pennsylvania mining town of Swoyersville, near Wilkes-Barre, where their father had settled in 1911 when he came to this country from Poland.

Walter and Mary Michaels had seven sons and a daughter before Walter dropped dead when he was 54, after twenty-five years in the mines.

One of their sons, Eddie, was killed at Guadalcanal. Their daughter Frances died. The two oldest brothers, Stanley and Tom, followed their father into the mines. They're retired now, with silicosis in their lungs. The third son, Joe, was the first to play football, followed by Jake, but Walt and Lou were the ones who made it big.

Walt went to Washington & Lee and later to the Cleveland Browns, where he was an All-NFL linebacker. Lou went to the University of Kentucky, where he was an All-America, and on to the Los Angeles Rams and the Pittsburgh Steelers before joining the Colts. Once, when Lou was a young offensive lineman with the Rams, he played against Walt.

"I had to screen him on one play," Lou recalls. "But if I had to hit him a downfield block, I would have fallen down."

Though six years apart in age, Walt and Lou had been very close. Their father had died when Lou, the baby of the family, was eleven. Since the other brothers had already married, Lou grew up idolizing Walt, who later guided him to Staunton Military Academy in Virginia and to Kentucky. Walt advised him on contract negotiations when the Rams drafted him in the first round. Now they were Super Bowl rivals.

"Two sons in the Super Bowl, two sons," Walt had said the previous Sunday when the Jets and Colts qualified. "How would you like to be Mrs. Michaels now?"

Mrs. Michaels was now 72, white-haired, but peppy. Of all her children, of all her twenty-five grandchildren, and of all her eight great-grandchildren, Walt and Lou were the ones she was thinking about most now. They had made her famous once before. She was selected as the Pro Football Mother of the Year. Next weekend she would arrive for the game and share her time with her two sons turned rivals.

"She's a great Polish lady," Walt said, "the kind they don't tell jokes about."

He remembers his father, whose last name was Majka, before it was Americanized to Michaels, and how his father taught him about discipline, how no one would have any respect for him until he was consistent, until he was himself.

"He understood only two things about football—hitting and winning," Walt says. "If you hit, you won. And if you won, you were successful. He won when he hit Ellis Island."

SUNDAY, JANUARY 5
"The Enormity of It All"

Throughout the nine-thirty mass at St. Pius X, a brown, modern-styled Catholic church a few blocks down Route A1A, Mark Smolinski glanced across at Don Shula, a few pews ahead of him. Shula had cut Smolinski from the Colts in 1963, and now, when the mass ended, the captain of the Jets' special teams moved quickly into the steady rain, glancing back to be sure the rival coach wasn't nearby.

"No hard feelings," Smolinski would say later. "I just didn't want to have to say hello to him."

The two teams were lodged about a mile apart, too close for the comfort of many players, such as Johnny Sample. He had attended the same mass, and when he returned to his room after breakfast at the Galt, his phone was ringing.

"John," a familiar voice announced. "The champions of the National Football League have arrived."

Sample had been expecting Lenny Lyles to call. They had been roommates as rookies with the Colts in 1958, and despite Sample's later travels with the Pittsburgh Steelers, the Washington Redskins, and the Jets, their friendship had flourished. Several months after the Super Bowl game, they would take their wives and children on a vacation together, but now they were rival cornerbacks. Lyles would be assigned to George Sauer, Jr., while Sample would be covering Willie Richardson.

"John," said Lyles on the phone, "I'm going to bring Willie over to meet you. He's some cat."

"You keep Willie away from here," Sample said. "I'll meet Willie next Sunday, not before."

"C'mon, John, you've got to get to know this cat. You'll like him. Willie is a nice guy, John."

"You keep him away from here," Sample repeated. "You know I won't be rough on somebody I like."

Being rough is Johnny Sample's style. Rough with his strength and rough with his mouth. Most cornerbacks are relatively slender, but he is a thickly muscled, 6-foot 1-inch tall, 204-pounder. At the age of 31, he no longer possessed blazing speed. But he used his strength to intimidate pass-receivers, and he used his mouth to remind them of it.

In between, he blessed himself with the sign of the cross, quickly, before each play.

For him, the Super Bowl game represented the culmination of a private crusade. He contended that he had been "blackballed" by the NFL. But Sample had wished for a different opponent than the Colts. He still had several close friends among his one-time teammates, especially Lyles, Johnny Unitas, Don Shinnick, and Dick Szymanski.

"Their owner, Carroll Rosenbloom," he has said, "arranged for me to buy the house I live in now. Saved me a lot of money. But the rest of the NFL, I hate 'em as bad as a dog biting my wife."

Ordinarily, Sample is among the friendliest members of the Jets. But now he had changed. Whenever he spoke about the NFL, his big brown eyes flashed in defiance, and he thrust his big jaw higher than usual. His shoulders swaggered slightly inside his Nehru jacket, and his stride appeared to have more purpose in his bell-bottomed slacks with silken pleats. His lime-green mod suit set him apart from the other players. When he appeared in the lobby, strangers stared at him. But his appearances were few.

"I want a single room," he had told John Free.

"And when your wife comes down," the traveling secretary said, "she'll move in with you. Is that correct?"

"No, the single room is for me."

"And another room for your wife?"

"No, she's going to stay at the Americana with the kids when she gets here. I'm staying here alone until after the game. I've got a lot of thinking to do in that room."

"I understand," Free said.

In his meditation, Johnny Sample realized he not only was a marked man, but *the* marked man. Joe Namath's comments had outraged some people, but Namath's situation was different. As a quarterback, his performance depended on his blockers and his receivers, and even on his runners. But a cornerback is all by himself. If he misses a coverage, it's a touchdown, and *he* is responsible. No alibi is possible. And because of his outspoken crusade against the NFL, he was the villain of this Super Bowl, just as Fred Williamson of the Kansas City Chiefs and Ben Davidson of the Oakland Raiders held the role in the previous two years.

Williamson, also a cornerback, had threatened Packer receivers with his karate chop.

"'The Hammer,' that's me," Williamson had declared. "I've broken thirty helmets."

But early in the final quarter of the first Super Bowl game, Williamson was flattened by Donny Anderson of the Packers on an end sweep. Knocked unconscious, Williamson played no more that day. After the game, Coach Vince Lombardi was asked why it took the Packers so long to get "The Hammer."

"Because," said Lombardi, smiling, "it took him that long to make a tackle."

The next year Davidson, a towering defensive end at 6-feet 8-inches and 285 pounds, had arrived with various credentials. He once had been cut by the Packers. He recently had swatted Namath, the impact spinning the quarterback's helmet across the sideline, fracturing his cheekbone and incurring a 15-yard penalty for unnecessary roughness. He also wore a twirled handlebar mustache and liked to ride a motorcycle. He had everything going for him— revenge, a reputation as a violent competitor, and the appearance of an executioner. But against the Packers, he played like a lamb.

"The Mustache," said Bob Skoronski, the Packer tackle who blocked him easily, "got trimmed."

And now Johnny Sample, with a reputation that combined the most controversial elements of Williamson and Davidson, had to prove that he could cover Richardson, one of the NFL's most respected flankers. Sample's reputation originated in the 1959 NFL championship game between the Colts and the New York Giants. He was covering Frank Gifford, now the CBS telecaster who then was interested in a career as a Hollywood actor. On an early play, Sample slammed Gifford across the sideline, the pass squirting incomplete. As they got up, Sample grinned.

"Hey, Hollywood," he told Gifford, "you're too pretty to be playing this game."

Gifford ignored him, trotting back to the huddle without a word or a glance. Gradually, the Giants built a 9–7 lead entering the final quarter. But at every opportunity, Sample, then in his second season, kept jabbering at Gifford, an old pro of stature.

"You're going to get mussed up," Sample said once, "and then they won't want you for movies."

"Stop running off at the mouth," Gifford finally snapped. "You've got a lot to learn, kid."

Years later, Sample confided, "That's when I knew I had him. When they get sore and answer you back, that's when you can tell you're getting to them. They get mad at me, and they try to do things to hurt me. They forget their patterns, and that's when I accomplish what I want, especially late in the game." That day Sample intercepted two of Charley Conerly's passes in the final quarter. He returned the first 24 yards to set up a touchdown. He returned the other 42 yards for a touchdown as the Colts rallied to win, 31–16.

He knew how to run with a football. He had run with it as a halfback at Maryland State, where he played both ways.

"On defense, I played left cornerback, same as now," he says. "Our coach, Vernon McCain, didn't believe in substitutions. You played sixty minutes. And you played without good equipment. Six good pairs of shoulder pads, that's all the team had, and you had to wait until you were a senior to get them. There were never enough hip pads to go around, and the ones they had were bulky with the buckles and straps. I never bothered with hip pads and thigh pads. To this day I don't wear 'em."

At the far end of their college field was a huge sign: Maryland State Hawks Always Win.

"The first thing we did at practice was to run down to that sign. We had to run around it to see it, but Coach McCain wanted every single player reading that sign every single day. It helped. In my four years there, we lost two games, and none in our conference. The practices lasted three hours, and they were harder than anything I've ever gone through, before or since. We would scrimmage on Friday before a game and on Monday after it. And if somebody got hurt, they'd let him lay there. They'd move the scrimmage downfield."

As talented as he was on offense, he had been influenced by advice from Paul Brown, then coaching the Cleveland Browns.

"He came to a banquet we had," Sample has said. "I remember he mentioned how if you want to make a good living and have a long career in the pros, be a defensive back. When I got drafted by the Colts, I had that in mind. They had good offensive backs like Lenny Moore, Alan Ameche, and L. G. Dupre, so I figured my best chance was on defense."

Sample was a seventh-round draft choice, but he was selected for the College All-Star team.

"The first guy from an all-Negro school ever named," he says proudly. "That was some honor."

The coach of the All-Star squad, Otto Graham, predicted to Weeb Ewbank, then the Colt coach, that Sample "won't make it." But after a quiet rookie season in 1958, Sample established himself as a cornerback and as a kickoff-return and punt-return runner. Two years later, during an exhibition game prior to the 1961 season, he antagonized Ewbank by fumbling a punt in the end zone.

"That's going to cost you one hundred dollars," Ewbank fumed.

"If it does, I'm going to have to go home," Sample replied. "I don't deserve to be fined for that."

"I think you do," Ewbank said. "Start packing."

Sample returned to Philadelphia, where he had been a basketball teammate of Wilt Chamberlain at Overbrook High School. A few days later, he was traded to the Steelers. He was selected as an All-NFL safetyman by United Press International that year. But after the 1962 season, he was traded to the Redskins.

"Buddy Parker told people I got drunk," Sample has said of the Steeler coach then. "I never had alcohol in my life."

After three seasons with the Redskins, his future was clouded by the appointment of Otto Graham as the new coach. Graham soon phoned Sample.

"You're making too much money for a defensive back," Graham said in the course of the conversation.

"And are *you* making too much money for a coach?" Sample retorted.

Shortly after that brief conversation, he was dealt to the Chicago Bears, but another salary dispute developed. He had been making a reported $40,000 with the Redskins, and when he asked for a raise to install his family in Chicago for the season, George Halas, then the gruff owner-coach of the Bears, was not about to pay that much money for a defensive back. Sample took his problem to Commissioner Pete Rozelle.

"You're a free agent," Rozelle decided.

"You mean I can sign with any team, in any league—NFL or AFL?"

"That's right. Any team. Any league."

Sample phoned another NFL office but, he says, "I was told that the word on me in the NFL was hands-off. I'd been blackballed." He then phoned Ewbank, who needed an experienced cornerback. His new career began. That meant new receivers to cover and a new notebook to keep. During his NFL seasons, he had maintained a rating system on each receiver. His ratings are on a 5-4-3-2-1 basis in five categories: speed, ability to run pass patterns, ability to go after the ball aggressively, blocking, and reaction to intimidation.

"The only one I've ever given a 5 in all categories," he has said, "is Lance Alworth of the San Diego Chargers."

But now, in the days before the Super Bowl, he needed to rate Willie Richardson, the All-NFL flanker in 1967. Before he left his Philadelphia home, Sample watched films of the late-season Colt-Packer game in his cellar with his buddy, Herb Adderley, the Packer cornerback.

Before the projector was turned on, he got out his old NFL notebook. He had covered Richardson occasionally before he became a starter.

"I had given him a 5 in speed," Sample disclosed later, "but he's not as fast now. I gave him a 3 in patterns and aggressiveness and a 2 in blocking and intimidation. Not too good."

After viewing the films, during which Richardson caught a touchdown pass with a perfectly timed leap behind Adderley in the corner of the end zone, Sample upgraded his ability in running his patterns.

"Especially the deep ones," Sample said.

The deep patterns, the ones that produce an instant touchdown, were what Johnny Sample had to stop. During the season, he had preserved a 23–20 victory over the Chargers with an interception at the 5-yard line in the final minute. Another interception, with which he dashed 36 yards for a touchdown, supplied the winning margin in a 25–21 triumph over the Buffalo Bills, but that had been on a sideline pattern, and his intuition had prepared him for it.

"I was waiting for that pass because Kay Stephenson," he said, referring to the Bills' quarterback, "had completed a couple like that on me in the last game last season when he was with the Chargers. We were way ahead, and I was playing loose. You don't forget something like that. I knew he hadn't. I could tell by the way he backed up that it would be a short pass. He has a big windup, like a baseball pitcher, so I had plenty of time to react"

In the AFL championship game, he didn't react as well. Fred Biletnikoff, the Raider flanker, outran him on a post pattern—a deep route toward the goalpost—for an early touchdown. When he came off the field, Sample was benched by Ewbank, who had considered not starting him. Sample later returned, and Biletnikoff caught no more touchdown passes. Ewbank had announced that Sample would open against the Colts, but the doubt had been created. Aging and tired, he might not be able to stay with Willie Richardson.

And whenever Johnny Sample was alone in his room, he thought about that and about how he could conquer that doubt.

Now, as he locked his door on the way to the noon meeting, Sample glanced up to see Emerson Boozer and Cornell Gordon strolling through the hallway.

"Card game after practice," Boozer said. "My room."

"I'm out," Johnny Sample said. "No cards for me."

Larry Grantham was talking with Paul Zimmerman of the New York *Post*. Suddenly, the linebacker glanced at his wristwatch. "Ten minutes to twelve," he said. "I've never been late for a meeting in nine years, and I'm not going to start now. Not this week."

In the darkness of the Imperial Room, the players were watching the Colts and the Vikings in the Western Conference title game.

The members of the Jet offensive unit continued to be unawed by the Colt defensive unit.

"If the Vikings had a passer, they could do something," a voice said. "But Joe Kapp isn't Joe Namath."

At the defensive end of the room, Walt Michaels was providing his personal sound track for the silent film. The essence of it was that the Colt offense wasn't that spectacular, that the Jet defense had controlled AFL offenses that were as good, if not better. But in his quiet way, Michaels had been sabotaging the NFL aura of superiority for several months, beginning the day after a Monday night game between the Packers and the Dallas Cowboys on national television that many Jets had watched.

"We've stopped the same plays that the Cowboys used," Michaels told his players, "and we've seen the Packer formations. The teams in the NFL haven't cornered the market on anything— not on strategy, not on talent, not on anything."

Now, in their third day of viewing the Colt offense, his players were beginning to believe him, and they were willing to believe him because they knew he had played in the NFL and they respected his opinion. But with all his subtle psychology, Walt Michaels realized that the one Colt who was better than anybody at his position in the AFL, the one Colt who had to be controlled, John Mackey, was the player who might destroy his unit. He was hoping to prod Jim Hudson into a maximum effort.

"Hey, Jim," he said when the screen went blank, "Mackey went to Syracuse, didn't he?"

Hudson, the quiet Texan, nodded, wondering what Walt Michaels was about to say to him next.

"Don't tell me," the defensive coach said, "that Texas can't beat Syracuse every time."

Softly, in the chant of a cheer, Joe Namath was talking to himself, perhaps subconsciously, as he entered the locker room at Fort Lauderdale Stadium.

"V-I-C-T-O-R-Y," the quarterback was saying in cadence. "Are we in? Well, I guess. Beaver Falls High School—yes, yes, yes . . . V-I-C-T-O-R-Y. Are we in? Well, I guess. Beaver Falls High School—yes, yes, yes!"

The rain had stopped, but Weeb Ewbank was outside, inspecting the condition of the field.

"The ground is still sloppy," he announced on returning to the locker room. "I don't want anybody cutting out there and maybe pulling a muscle. We'll do some wind sprints and some 30-yard relays, but just straight-ahead stuff, just to break a sweat. I don't want anybody doing anything foolish out there now."

In the relays, the members of the offensive unit raced against the members of the defensive unit. The offense lost.

"The defense always wins," Bill Baird, the free safety-man, said in the locker room. "The defense has faster players."

Down at the Orange Bowl stadium in Miami, where the Super Bowl would be played next Sunday, the Dallas Cowboys would defeat the Minnesota Vikings, 17–13, in the NFL Playoff Bowl, but the most concerned spectator was Mark Duncan, the supervisor of officials in Commissioner Pete Rozelle's office.

Duncan is responsible for the condition of the playing field in post-season games, and the Orange Bowl turf, soft from the morning rain, had turned to glop. But that night, George Toma, the groundskeeper for the Kansas City Chiefs and reputedly the best one in pro football, would arrive in Miami.

"It's a mess right now," Duncan would tell the Commissioner that night, "but George Toma will fix it up."

Al Atkinson had been excused from the Jet workout. He had eased into the warm, bubbly water of the oval aluminum whirlpool bath to treat his stretched calf muscles. Now, as he sat there, immersed to the waist, he casually read a paperback copy of *In Cold Blood*.

"Where are you?" a passerby asked.

"Just after they're hitch-hiking," he said, meaning the two killers in the novel. "They're about to clobber the guy who picked them up, and he stops to pick up somebody else. It's great."

"That's one of the best scenes."

"That and in the beginning," he said, "when the four people in the house get their heads blown off." Spoken like a middle linebacker.

Before the season began, a poll of AFL players by *Sport* magazine had included a "most underrated player" category. The winner had been Al Atkinson, and despite the ascent of the Jets, he had continued to remain relatively unobtrusive in what is usually a glamor position.

"But I'd rather be underrated than overrated," he often said, "because when you're overrated, you're on the way out."

Instead, at the age of 25, he was on the way up with his boyish face and quiet, almost shy manner, the antithesis of the usual image of a middle linebacker. Even his name added to his colorless reputation. Ray Nitschke of the Packers, that's a name that sounds like a middle linebacker's should. So does Dick Butkus of the Chicago Bears and Tommy Nobis of the Atlanta Falcons.

In contrast, the name Al Atkinson has a softer ring.

But there is nothing soft about his style. Jim Hudson calls him "Hombre," a Texan's term of respect. But Atkinson became a Jet almost by accident. While he attended Villanova in 1964, he had been drafted by the Colts, his favorite team as a boy. But he also had been drafted by the Buffalo Bills. He chose to sign with the AFL team.

"They drafted me in the third round," he has said, "and the Colts took me in the sixth, so I figured the Bills wanted me more."

Not for long. At the time the Bills were the AFL champions, and they would successfully defend their title in 1965. Their linebackers were solid. In the final cut at training camp, Atkinson was put on waivers, and the Jets claimed him. As usually happens to a rookie who hasn't had time to learn his new team's system, he was assigned to the special teams—the kickoff and punting units. On those reckless dashes downfield, a player reveals how tough, or how timid, he is.

Atkinson had the most brutal task. His responsibility was to bust the wedge of blockers surrounding the ballcarrier.

In one of his first games, the 230-pound rookie smashed through on kickoffs for five unassisted tackles. Soon after that, he got his chance at middle linebacker. The incumbent, Wahoo McDaniel, who was part Choctaw, had been a folk hero to many Jet fans in the pre-Namath era, but his career was on the decline. In a few months he departed in the expansion draft that stocked the Miami Dolphins for the 1966 season, and Al Atkinson was established as the regular middle linebacker.

Not that it was easy. At Villanova he had been a defensive tackle. He would have to learn pass-coverage.

"But now," says Walt Michaels, "when I look at films of a game, I can't hardly ever call him for a serious mistake. He's a steady, dependable player. Some linebackers like to gamble, but I don't want mine to. Gambling linebackers might make nine great plays, but the tenth is a touchdown, and that's no good. Al Atkinson might not be spectacular, but he doesn't make that big mistake that can cost us a touchdown. And he's a tough kid. He's one of the toughest players we've got."

Weeb Ewbank found that out during a 1966 game when Atkinson wobbled to the sideline.

"Maybe you better come out for the next series," the coach told him. "I'll get somebody else in there."

"The hell you will," Atkinson snapped. "I'll tell you when I have to come out. I'll be all right."

That same thin-lipped look was on his face now as he climbed out of the whirlpool bath.

"I can't understand how most of the writers from NFL cities underrate us," he said. "I had a phone call this morning from a writer

I know in Philadelphia, a good friend of mine. We were talking about our chances, and he said, 'I've seen your league a couple of times on television. It reminds me of two-hand touch.' It's lucky he said it on the phone. If he'd said it to my face, I might've popped him."

In his annoyance, he sailed his copy of *In Cold Blood* into his locker.

When the buses turned into the driveway at the Galt, the kids were waiting, as they were every afternoon. There were about two dozen of them, their eyes searching through the tinted-glass windows of the buses as they rolled to a stop.

"Joe's on this one," a youngster shouted.

When the quarterback slouched onto the sidewalk, the kids ignored the other players and surrounded him, waving pictures and autograph books and slips of paper.

"You kids betting on the Jets?" he asked.

"I am," one said. "I bet a whole dollar."

Four or five other voices announced that they were wagering on the Jets, and suddenly the quarterback stopped signing his name and looked down at them.

"If you lose any money," he said, quite seriously, "come here after the game, and I'll reimburse you."

In a nearby restaurant, Bill Mathis, Curley Johnson, and Pete Lammons had ordered dinner. On their table was a lighted candle and a basket with two loaves of bread wrapped in paper. Mathis thoughtlessly lifted one of the paper-wrapped loaves above the candle and the paper burst into flames, startling his companions.

"What the hell!" said Lammons, pulling away.

Mathis succeeded in tapping out the flame with his cloth napkin. But moments later, in taking the other loaf of bread, the same thing happened. Seeing the flames this time, their waitress poured a glass of water on the blazing paper.

"They ought to wrap the bread in *The Wall Street Journal* here," Johnson said. "You wouldn't burn that."

Bill Mathis is a prosperous stockbroker with the Wall Street firm of Cogan, Berlind, Weill, and Levitt, and he moves through the big city with aplomb. But in 1960, when he was a rookie with the original Titan team, he was a straw-haired halfback from Clemson who was leery of the skyscrapers and the smooth-talking city slickers.

"I had been in New York only once before," he recalled. "I was 11, and I went there for a vacation with my parents, and we stayed at the Manhattan Hotel. When I joined the Titans, that was the only place I remembered, so I went there. I stayed there all season, taking the subway up to the Polo Grounds and coming back."

Soon, with his courtly manners, the 220-pound Mathis was among the most popular Titans, and the most skilled. So much so that, because he had never been cut by an NFL team, many Giant loyalists were willing to concede that *maybe* he could have made their established New York team.

Midway in the 1966 season, Emerson Boozer began to emerge as a breakaway threat, and Mathis no longer was the starting halfback. But he played much of every game because of his flawless proficiency in protecting Joe Namath from blitzing linebackers and his dependability as a short-yardage runner and occasional pass-receiver.

During the 1968 season, Weeb Ewbank didn't dare risk Boozer's surgical knee in a game against the Houston Oilers in the Shea Stadium mud. Mathis scored the two Jet touchdowns in the 26–7 victory that virtually assured the team of its first divisional title.

Equally appreciated was his stock-market advice. He recently had suggested that his teammates invest in Glen Alden, a conglomerate, selling at about fifteen dollars a share. Since then, it had gone up to about eighteen dollars, and some of the Jets had prospered with him. Now as the waitress replaced the water-soaked tablecloth, Curley Johnson stared at big, blond Bill Mathis who played football for fun, not for money.

"I hope," Johnson said, "the stock exchange never has to operate with candles."

With his faraway preoccupied look, John Free was hurrying through the Galt lobby as he stared at a rooming list. John Free always seems to be staring at a rooming list. But as he headed towards the elevators, a friend complimented the traveling secretary on the casual elegance of his white cardigan sweater.

"Thank you," he said. "Some guys got it, and some guys don't. I've got part of it."

Joe Namath and Jim Hudson were standing near the bar in Jimmy Fazio's restaurant when a big, black-haired, thick-eyebrowed man approached them.

"Namath," the man growled, "Lou Michaels."

The quarterback had known about Lou Michaels, the Colts' 32-year-old place-kicker, for more than a decade. His older brother Frank had roomed with Michaels at the University of Kentucky, but now the 6-foot 2-inch, 250-pound Colt, the brother of the Jet defensive coach, thrust his jaw toward the slouch-shouldered spokesman for the AFL.

"You're doing a lot of talking," Michaels said.

"There's a lot to talk about," Namath answered. "We're going to kick hell out of your team."

"Haven't you heard of the word modesty, Joseph?"

Aware of the incendiary atmosphere, Hudson suggested to Namath that they go to a table for dinner. But when they sat down, Michaels and his companion, Colt guard Dan Sullivan, joined them.

"You still here?" Namath said.

"Damn right I'm still here," Michaels said. "I want to hear all you got to say."

"I'm going to pick you apart."

"You're going to find it hard throwing out of a well."

"My blockers will give me time."

"I never heard Johnny Unitas or Bobby Layne talk like that."

"I believe that."

"Even if we get in trouble, we'll send in the master," Michaels said, meaning Unitas.

"I hope you do," Namath said, smiling, "because that'll mean the game is too far gone."

"Too far what!" Michaels snapped.

"Excuse me," Namath said. "I want to say hello to a few friends of mine."

Michaels was fuming.

"Don't pay any attention to what Joe says," Hudson said. "You've got to understand him." Namath soon returned.

"Suppose we kick hell out of your team?" Michaels resumed. "Just suppose we do that. What then, Namath?"

"I'll tell you what I'll do," the quarterback replied. "I'll sit in the middle of the field and I'll cry."

They all laughed.

After that, the belligerence vanished. The two Colts and the two Jets talked easily, the way rival football players usually do, and slowly, Lou Michaels began to understand the rival quarterback. When the check came, Namath grabbed it and peeled a hundred-dollar bill off his green-and-black wad.

"You got a ride back to the hotel?" Namath said.

"No," said Michaels, "but we'll jump in a cab."

"Don't be silly," Namath said. "I'll drop you."

When the two Colts got out of the car in the driveway of the Statler Hilton, they thanked Joe Namath and walked toward the hotel entrance.

"You know something," Michaels said to Sullivan, "he's a helluva guy."

In the dim light of the Rum House, on a high stool at the far end of the bar, George Sauer, Jr., was holding a brown paper sack against his yellow windbreaker. Inside it was an opened bag of Fritos. He had already taken out a can of Planters Peanuts, twirled it open and placed it on the bar. He had purchased them as snacks for his room, but now, in his midnight hunger, he was munching away as he sipped a glass of beer.

"I'm just starting to realize the enormity of it all," he said to a companion. "It's just starting to sink in."

With his black horned-rim glasses, long blond hair, and tender manner, he resembles a studious scientist more than a split end, but in reality he is both. He runs his pass patterns precisely. He practices incessantly. When he observes in films the defensive back who will cover him, he dissects his ability, move by move. His playbook is filled with significant notations on his personal involvement and experience.

Physical instincts guide most pro football players but with George Sauer, Jr., his mentality is as important, if not more important, than his muscle. He reads avidly. In his hip pocket now was a paperback copy of *The Myth of Sisyphus*, by Albert Camus, the French dramatist, novelist, and essayist who was the 1957 Nobel Prize winner for literature. In the months to come, he would attempt a novel himself.

"My problem this week," he was saying now in his thoughtful way, "is not to be overwhelmed by the situation, by the importance of the game, by the way it's spread all over the newspapers. And like today, when we got back from practice, the kids were waiting for us to get autographs. It suddenly struck me *why* I'm here. I began to realize that this is the biggest game in pro football, *all* pro football."

He munched on some peanuts and sipped his glass of beer.

"My problem this week," he said, "is keeping my cool."

But that always had been a problem for him because he had to grow up with his father's name. For more than three decades, when football followers thought of George Sauer, they thought of the big, friendly man who had been an All-America fullback at the University of Nebraska, who had played with the Green Bay Packers, who had been head coach at Navy and at Baylor, who had been elected to the college football Hall of Fame and who now, as the Jets' director of player personnel, scouted college players.

But now most football followers associated the name George Sauer with his 25-year-old son.

"As a boy, my name made me pretty self-conscious because I developed slowly," the younger Sauer acknowledged. "I had started school in Maryland when my father was coaching Navy and when we moved to Waco, where Baylor is located, somehow I was a year younger than most of the other kids in my class. At that age a year makes a big difference. When I was in junior high school, I was really behind them. I never got a football letter in junior high school. In fact, I didn't get a letter in high school until my junior year, and that was a gift. I was a halfback, but I never got in on offense. I played a few games on defense and ran down under a few kickoffs, but they lettered everyone, so I was lucky.

"The next year I played both ways, as a split end and as a safety, and I made all-state. But until then, I had gone through the anguish of being a football player. I had run track and my coach, Wayne Gardner, who was an assistant football coach, kept after me to play football. He kept telling me that nothing is going to come quickly, and psychologically that lifted me."

His father never had pushed him toward football, for which he is grateful.

"Now that I think about it," he has said, "I have to admire his restraint. I see how hard other fathers push their sons in sports, but that never happened to me. My father never set goals for me. Understanding might be the first act of love, and he understood that I was playing against his name. I never was ridiculed or the object of much sarcasm from my peers, but I felt it."

His father had tossed a football with him in their backyard in Waco, where young George remembers the trees.

"We had around twelve trees in that backyard. Mostly fruit trees. Pear and apricot and peach trees, and we had a big ol' hackberry tree, and sometimes my father would throw the ball close to the trees, and I'd bounce off 'em after I caught it, and I remember my mother telling my father one time, 'With his hands, he should be an end.' And up here, when I catch a pass, sometimes it's like I was still bouncing off those trees in our big ol' backyard in Waco—except that now those trees are chasing me."

Over the last three seasons, he was chased more often than any pass-receiver in pro football.

As a rookie in 1965, he didn't establish himself as a starter until mid-season. But beginning in 1966, he caught a total of 204 passes in three seasons, compared to 193 for Lance Alworth of the San Diego Chargers, and to 190 for Charlie Taylor of the Washington Redskins. And he caught them with a contact lens to correct 20/200 vision in his right eye. His left eye has perfect 20/20 vision.

Since a split end usually lines up on the left side, his right eye is the first one to pick up the flight of the ball on an inside pass pattern.

"After I started to use the contact lens in 1966," he has said, "I realized that my depth perception hadn't been as accurate as it should be, especially on long passes. The short passes hadn't given me much trouble, but I had been having trouble on long ones. Now they're clearer."

After finishing second to Alworth in the AFL with 63 receptions in 1966, he led the league in 1967 with 75. Entering the 1968 season finale, he was leading again. But Alworth passed him to win the title, 68 to 66, when Sauer was limited to two receptions. Not that it concerned him.

"Suppose I'd caught a lot of passes," he explained later, "and taken some unnecessary chances and got hurt. I'm out of the championship game. The thought of it would've haunted me for the rest of my life."

Instead, he was a formidable factor in the championship victory with seven receptions in a duel with Willie Brown of the Raiders, the AFL's premier cornerback. Equally important, he had avoided injury and now, as he sat on the bar stool and sipped beer and munched a Frito, he looked ahead to his confrontation with Lenny Lyles, the experienced Colt cornerback.

"Coming back on the bus today," he said, "Johnny Sample filled me in a little on his man Lenny Lyles."

As devoted as was Sample's friendship with Lyles, his first loyalty this week was to his teammates.

"Lyles likes to go with the first fake, and he hits hard," Sauer said, "but he's not a cheap-shot guy."

Among the pros, a cheap-shot is a euphemism for dirty football tactics, abhorred by quality players.

"But if he gives me a cheap shot, I'll know that he thinks that he's got to intimidate me in order to stop me. If he gives me a cheap shot, I'll know he's afraid of me."

With that, he pushed away his empty glass and got up to leave.

"You had four or five beers," his companion said. "That's a lot for you."

"They help me to get to sleep," he said. "Otherwise I'd be awake all night."

MONDAY, JANUARY 6

"Namath Can Say Whatever the Hell He Wants"

Outside, it was drizzling. But shortly before ten o'clock in the locker room at Fort Lauderdale Stadium, most of the Jets were putting on the white uniforms they would wear in the Super Bowl game. This was Photo Day, one of the command performances for the participants, and the players had been told to be available for newspaper photographers and television crews. But not all of them were there.

"I wonder," one of the players said, "when Joe will arrive."

About an hour earlier, a wake-up call had rung in the Governor's Suite, and Jim Hudson had responded. As he moped about, getting dressed, he jostled his roommate.

"Let's go, Joe," he said. "Got to get up."

"Get up for what?" the quarterback said, half asleep. "We're off today. No practice today. No meeting."

"It's picture day, ten o'clock, pictures."

"If they want pictures of me, they're going to have to take 'em later than ten o'clock."

With that the quarterback went back to sleep.

Across the patio, in room 368, Matt Snell and Emerson Boozer were sleeping. Their phone had rung earlier, but they had ignored it.

"We forgot about the picture day," Boozer would say later. "We thought it was another silly call."

But now, out at the stadium, the cameramen were annoyed at the absence of the quarterback. Overhearing one of them complain, Rocky Rochester approached equipment manager Bill Hampton.

"Give me an extra number 12 jersey," Rocky said.

Moments later, he strutted into the center of the locker room, his belly out, the "12" all too obvious. His teammates howled with laughter. But realizing that he needed another prop, he grabbed a hairbrush and flattened his thin, brown hair around his ears.

"All right, boys," he announced, "get your cameras ready."

He didn't fool any of the cameramen, but his teammates enjoyed his attempted disguise. Somehow it seemed to take the sting out of Namath's absence. Very few photographers appeared aware that Snell and Boozer hadn't shown. On the field, the photographers had grouped the regulars into various units—the offensive linemen, the pass-receivers, the defensive linemen, the linebackers, the defensive backs. The other players were being ignored. John Neidert, a reserve linebacker, shook his head.

"Unless there's a photographer here from the *Akron Beacon-Journal*," he said with a laugh, referring to his hometown newspaper, "nobody will be taking my picture."

At the Hilton Plaza on Miami Beach, a young blonde accompanied by Jim Marooney, the NBC unit manager, walked into the press room where Ed Weisman, the television network's sports publicity man, who died three months later, was waiting to open an information desk. Marooney had hired the receptionist from an employment service.

"Here she is," Marooney said.

"Hi," the blonde said. "My name is Heidi."

"You're kidding," Weisman said.

"No, sir," she said. "My name really is Heidi—Heidi DuDec."

"Jim told you to say that."

"No, sir. That's my name."

"Somebody put you up to it," Weisman said, recalling the furor over the showing of the children's classic "Heidi" instead of the final minutes of the Jets-Raiders regular-season game.

"No," she said. "Honestly."

"All right, Heidi," said Weisman. "Sit down, and I'll explain your duties. First of all you have to wear this button."

Weisman handed her a big white button, with blue words: "Heidi Loves The Super Bowl."

Marooney smiled. "I have to confess, Eddie," he said. "They showed me a list of about thirty names, and when I saw a Heidi on it, I said, I don't care if she can't type, that's the girl.' So here she is."

The phone on the desk rang, and Heidi was working.

As he dressed after the picture-taking, kick-return specialist Earl Christy slid two twenty-dollar bills into his pocket.

"That's all I got," he said. "I lost my wallet, and I had to borrow this from John Free."

"Run one back all the way Sunday," somebody said, "and you won't have to pay him back."

Throughout the season, Christy had been promising people that he would run back a kickoff or a punt all the way for a touchdown. He never did. He came close in Buffalo, being bounced out of bounds on the 3-yard line, but close isn't the same as scoring. He almost had scored with an interception as a defensive back late in the 47–31 victory over the Boston Patriots, and he had celebrated with a leaping, jumping, waving dance that delighted his teammates.

His personality delighted them all the time. Quick to laugh, he enjoyed a special rapport with Joe Namath.

"Joe," he once said as the quarterback hobbled stiffly out of the trainer's room, "you're a physical hazard."

At 5-feet 11-inches tall and 195 pounds, Christy had the most hazardous job in football himself—returning kickoffs and punts with a horde of opposing tacklers thundering toward him. And when tackled, he would bounce to his feet, snatch off his helmet, and run to the sideline, his balding head there for all to see. At the age of 25, he was quite bald. But the same reckless spirit that enabled him to return kicks also enabled him to ignore the embarrassment of baldness that some players try to hide under their helmets.

"Man," he was saying now in the locker room, "I just *have* to run one back all the way Sunday."

He grew up in Perryman, Maryland, attended Maryland State College, then joined the Jets as a free agent.

"Everybody back home, all they talk about is the Colts," he said. "If we lose, I'm in trouble."

Most of the Colts had assembled for their team meeting when Lou Michaels arrived. Somehow the news of his confrontation with Namath had circulated among his teammates.

"We heard about it, Lou," one of them began.

"Heard about what?" Michaels said, wondering.

"About how you let Namath buy you off with that $100 bill," another said.

"He's a good guy," Michaels said, "a good guy."

"Then how come you were ready to bust him in the mouth?" another asked.

"It wasn't like that," Michaels said.

"Joe Namath," another said, "is the 837th guy that Lou has challenged, but if Lou had belted him, he would be only the 37th guy that Lou actually hit."

The absence of the three Jet stars, notably Namath, was a disaster to the public-relations men in Commissioner Pete Rozelle's headquarters at the Hilton Plaza. Their job is to organize cooperation between newsmen and the members of the competing teams. But the Super Bowl's most newsworthy individual had ignored the important Photo Day. When it was reported to Jim Kensil, the

Commissioner's executive assistant and former publicity chief, he phoned Weeb Ewbank.

"Those three players," Kensil ordered, "have to be available for pictures before tomorrow's workout."

Ewbank agreed. He hadn't planned a serious workout anyway. His players would just loosen up. And since Namath wasn't scheduled to throw, the quarterback would have time for the cameramen. But even before Kensil's phone call, Ewbank had decided to fine his three absentees fifty dollars each.

At the Statler Hilton, in the elegant dimness of the Don Quixote room, Don Shula was about to meet the press.

"Namath didn't show up for Photo Day?" the Colts' coach repeated, astounded. "What the hell is Weeb doing?"

Shula was wearing a Colt blue cardigan sweater over a white turtleneck dickey. He munched on a hamburger between questions. Husky and trim at 38, he appeared capable of playing in an emergency. He had been a defensive back with the Browns, Colts (four seasons under Ewbank), and Redskins, but he never was a star. He distinguished himself as a defensive aide with the Detroit Lions, and when Ewbank was discharged, he replaced him. During his six seasons, the Colts compiled a 63–18–3 record. To appreciate that record, the Packers posted a 58–21–1 record during the first six years of Vince Lombardi's regime.

More pertinent to the Super Bowl game, the Colts had won twenty-eight of their last thirty games with Shula on the sideline, including the NFL championship game and the Western Conference title game.

"We like to think," Shula often says, "that good coaching is something that occurs on the *day* of the game. Many coaches can organize a good game plan, but their ability to make an instant decision is what makes a coach."

Now, as he sipped a glass of milk after finishing his hamburger, he was asked his reaction to what he had seen of Joe Namath in viewing films of the Jet games. Shula began to rattle off comments, discussing Namath:

"He has a quick release . . .

"His vision downfield is good. He backpedals a lot more than quarterbacks in our league do . . .

"He'll unload the ball . . .

"He has a deep drop, but he has what we call fast feet, the ability to get back quickly . . .

"He has a strong, accurate arm . . .

"He's been with his receivers for four seasons, and they team up real well, Earl Morrall has been with our receivers only four months . . . the Jet offense is a lot like our team's . . . he's a lot like Sonny Jurgensen, a lot like Norm Van Brocklin was . . ."

Then he added his only comment with a negative trace.

"But he hasn't been throwing against the defenses that Earl has been throwing against."

When he mentioned Morrall, somebody asked him for his reaction to Namath's comparison of Morrall and Lamonica.

"I don't know how Namath can rap Earl," Shula replied. "After all, Earl's number one in the NFL. He's thrown all those touchdown passes. He's thrown for a great percentage without using dinky flare passes. And he's been voted the Player of the Year in our league. Earl has had a great year for us, and we're proud of him. Anyone who doesn't give him the credit he deserves is wrong."

The veins in his neck had thickened, and his square-jawed face suddenly betrayed his controlled anger.

"But I guess," the coach said, a rising edge in his voice, "Namath can say whatever the hell he wants."

The phone rang in John Free's room. Johnny Sample was calling the traveling secretary.

"John," the cornerback said, anxiously, "I've had forty tickets for the game stolen out of my room. Tickets I'd sold through my agency back home. People were supposed to pick them up from me down here."

"That's terrible," Free said.

"Do me a favor," Sample said. "Call the police for me."

"Certainly," Free replied.

When he put down the phone, Free wondered momentarily why Sample hadn't reported the burglary himself. Then he realized that in the South, a black person doesn't expect much cooperation from the police. Free's call produced an immediate response. Within minutes, a policeman was accompanying Free to Sample's room.

"Please be careful in handling this case," Free explained to the policeman. "You're dealing with one of the most volatile players we have."

Sample reported the details of the burglary. Throughout the week, the police would contact Sample daily on their progress in recovering the tickets. The cornerback obtained twenty-nine more, but the original forty were never located.

Freda Gordon, tiny and slim, had arranged a birthday party for her husband Cornell, 28 today. To make it a surprise, she had assigned a few players to detain him downstairs until the cake and a bowl of orange punch were delivered to the room. She and several guests had assembled there. Suddenly the door opened, and Cornell strolled in.

"The cake's behind me," he said, his usually dead-pan face splitting into a grin.

Moments later, a room-service waiter wheeled in a big flat cake, with white frosting and green decorations as if it were a football field. With it was the punch. There was a chorus of "Happy Birthday," then Cornell opened his wife's present, a black turtleneck sweater. Soon the cake and punch were passed around.

In the room were several Jets, including Gerry Philbin, Randy Beverly, Johnny Sample, Bill Baird, Winston Hill, Earl Christy, and

Verlon Biggs. But mingling with them was a stranger, Roy Hilton of the Colts, a substitute defensive end. Hilton had played with Biggs at Jackson State in Mississippi, and he was visiting him.

"I think we'll spike your punch, Roy," said Freda, smiling.

Hilton smiled back, then somebody suggested a toast to the Super Bowl. Lifting their glasses, they sipped their punch. Then one of the Jets turned to Hilton.

"After we win next Sunday," he said to the Colt, "come over for champagne."

"When we win," Roy Hilton said, casually confident, "you have my invitation."

Across the nation, at College Hospital in Santa Barbara, California, a doctor was explaining to Jimmy "The Greek" Snyder that tests that weekend had disclosed an abdominal obstruction.

"We're going to operate tomorrow morning," the doctor said.

"The sooner the better," Jimmy said. "The game's Sunday."

Several letters were in Weeb Ewbank's morning mail. Accompany-ing one of them were three neatly diagrammed plays.

"Dear Coach: Attached are three plays drawn for what I term The Flying 'I' formation. This formation can be shifted into or shifted out of as you see fit. The main idea is the confusion factor. Baltimore has never seen your team run or pass from this formation. If you can use it, we can discuss terms later. It's no crazier than the other plays or formations you probably get."

Ewbank laughed, as he tossed the letter into a nearby desk drawer.

"It'd confuse the Colts," he said, "but it would confuse us worse."

Near the pool, several players were enjoying their last free after-noon. Joe Namath was up by now, and he was needling Paul Crane.

"You see a linebacker this size," the quarterback said, "you know he's tough, you know he had to play at Alabama."

Paul Crane played with Namath on two national championship teams at the University of Alabama. He was an All-America center. He's from Prichard, Alabama, outside Mobile, but with his firm face and soft 'Bama drawl, he was born a hundred years too late. He belongs at Bull Run, wearing a gray Confederate officer's uniform and carrying a sword. He is used mostly as the center on the punting unit and on other special teams, but if one of the regular linebackers is hurt, he plays, at 205 pounds. It would be difficult to find a slimmer linebacker among the pros.

"When I hit 'em, I slice 'em," Crane replied, smiling. "When I hit 'em, they take 'em off on two stretchers."

"The first time you tried to tackle Cookie Gilchrist," Namath said, "he ran right up over the top of you."

Gilchrist, a 250-pound fullback who spent most of his AFL career with Buffalo, had stampeded bigger players.

"No, he didn't do that," Crane said. "But I'll tell you what he did do. He was going down the sidelines about a foot inside, and I hit him the best lick I could. I knocked him about six inches outside, and he kept on going."

They both laughed.

Paul Crane is a member of the Fellowship of Christian Athletes, a national organization. When the Jets say their team prayer in a locker room before a game, Crane naturally leads them. At a quick glance, he does not appear to be Joe Namath's kind of guy but they have that Alabama bond between them. One night he stopped by Namath's apartment in New York. Several other people were there, including a few loud-mouths who depend on obscenities to complete their vocabulary.

"All right," Namath whispered to the loud-mouths, "change your language while this guy is here."

And they did. Now, as the players around the pool continued their conversation, the language was as pure as the afternoon sunlight.

When Earl Morrall returned from the Colts' Photo Day, his wife, Jane, was in their room at the Statler Hilton. She noticed two cellophane packages of cheese crackers in his hands.

"You don't usually eat those," she said.

"I never got a chance to have lunch," the 34-year-old quarterback said. "Too many writers wanted to talk to me."

"That's the price you have to pay for fame."

"I'll pay it," Earl Morrall said. "I'll pay it."

The night before, Pete Lammons had been sitting in the Rum House with a beautiful blonde. Now, in the quiet of the sunny afternoon, the Jet tight end was relaxing on a chaise longue out by the beach when a companion congratulated him on his taste in girls.

"Yeah," the big bachelor said, smiling. "She's all right. She's *really* all right."

She isn't the only one. With his good looks, blond Pete Lammons resembles Paul Hornung, who never had trouble getting a date, not even in Green Bay, Wisconsin. When Lammons is in New York, he swings through the East Side spots with as much finesse as Joe Namath, although not with quite as much flair. In a football uniform, Lammons operates the same way, quietly and efficiently.

And ruggedly. As he proved early in the season following a torn muscle in his right leg.

"That's a bad one," Dr. Jim Nicholas warned him. "You might be out three or four weeks."

Several days later, Lammons was running. When the Jets went against the San Diego Chargers on Saturday night, he was in uniform on the sideline, pestering Weeb Ewbank to let him play. In the closing minutes, the Jets were trailing, but they had a fourth down on the Charger 1-yard line.

"I can block," Lammons pleaded. "I can't hurt my leg in a straight-ahead block."

Ewbank relented. Moments later, Lammons was among the blockers who enabled Emerson Boozer to score the winning touchdown of a 23–20 victory. In the locker room later, Dr. Nicholas approached the 6-foot 3-inch, 228-pounder from Jacksonville, Texas.

"Peter," the doctor said, "you are a medical phenomenon."

Of all the Jet casualties in recent seasons, Lammons is perhaps the quickest healer—and the quickest to reject surgery. His left knee has bothered him for several years, but he has refused to submit to Dr. Nicholas's suggestion that an operation would alleviate the situation.

"It hurts when I'm sitting down or walking on it a lot," he has said, "and I can't always bend it back. But I don't like to get cut on."

His fear of hospitals presumably began when he was about 2 years old in his east Texas hometown. He toppled off the roof of a two-story building and landed head first on cement. He had a concussion and laceration over his left eye.

"I don't remember it, or being in the hospital," he says, "but I guess that's when I started to dislike hospitals."

At the age of 7, he was hospitalized again with scarlet fever. But his most memorable experience occurred when he was at the University of Texas, where he was a linebacker as well as the tight end. In a game, a fellow linebacker, Tommy Nobis, accidently collided with Lammons. Nobis's knee jammed into Lammons's thigh. By the time the game ended, Lammons's right leg was black and blue and the team physician ordered him into the hospital.

"I didn't want to go," Lammons recalls. "But he told me it'd just be for overnight. The next day, he wouldn't let me out. My leg had hemorrhaged inside, and if I wasn't in the hospital, I might've had to have it amputated. I was lucky, but I still don't like hospitals. I played the next game anyway."

At Texas, he played in three bowl games. The 1963 Longhorns were national champions. During the Orange Bowl game that followed the 1964 season, Lammons intercepted two passes thrown by the Alabama quarterback, Joe Namath. Now he was *catching* his passes. As a rookie in 1966, he caught 41 for 565 yards. In 1967, he nearly repeated the performance—with 45 for 515. During the 1968 season Lammons caught 32 for 400 yards. In the AFL championship game, he caught one of Namath's three touchdown passes.

But a tight end must block, too, and against the Colts, he would be operating mostly against linebacker Mike Curtis.

"He's good," Lammons was saying now, sprawled on the beach chair. "He has to be good or he wouldn't have made the All-NFL team. But he can be blocked. Anybody can be blocked. He's no superman."

"Not like you," needled his companion.

"That's right," Lammons replied, winking. "Not many of us left."

"By the way, when are you getting married?"

"The twelfth," Lammons replied, seriously.

"The twelfth of what?"

"The twelfth of never," he said, laughing. "No use rushin' into somethin' like that."

About three miles off the shore of Fort Lauderdale, two chartered fishing yachts bobbed lazily.

Aboard one were Matt Snell, Verlon Biggs, and Jeff Richardson. On the other, perhaps 100 yards away, were Winston Hill and his wife, Carolyn, John Dockery, and Mike Stromberg. Moments earlier, Hill had been jolted when his bait was swallowed by a huge hammerhead shark.

"Look at him, Winnie," yelled Dockery. "He must be 7 feet long."

"And he must go 250," said Stromberg, "almost as big as you are."

Hill wasn't talking. He was too busy holding on to his bent pole. Soon the shark was alongside the yacht, but it was too heavy to drag aboard.

"Take us over to the other boat," Hill said to their skipper. "We've got to display this one."

Before their departure, each of the players had agreed to put up ten dollars as a prize for the boat catching the biggest fish. But now, as Hill, Dockery, and Stromberg motioned to the shark, the rival fisherman balked.

"No good," Snell shouted. "It has to be an edible fish."

"Nobody stipulated that," Hill screamed. "Just the biggest."

Snell knew that, of course, and he cackled. Biggs and Richardson also surrendered. Before they returned to the yacht basin, they caught several king mackerel. As payment to their rivals on the other yacht, six of them were kept for dinner that night at the Galt. Most of the ten-dollar prize money was awarded to the chef. Snell kept the largest mackerel, a 27-pounder, to be mounted, and Hill would arrange to have his huge shark mounted.

For a few hours at least, Winston Hill had been able to forget about Ordell Braase.

The game plan had been completed. It would be mimeographed and fastened inside folders, like a thesis. But each of the coaches and each of the quarterbacks also received typewritten instructions. Betty Spencer, the wife of the offensive line coach, had volunteered to type it.

"It's two pages," she said. "I thought it would only be one."

"It usually is," her husband replied. "But this is a *big* game."

In the lobby, two Jets, Sam Walton and Harvey Nairn, were waiting for an elevator to take them to the room they shared. When it arrived, they strolled inside, the metal floor vibrating under Walton's 276-pound body. Four days earlier he had turned 26, quite old for a rookie. He had been a third-round choice from East

Texas State, and he had started every game of the regular season at right tackle for the Jets' offense. He had replaced one of the most popular Jets, huge Sherman Plunkett.

The first day of training camp, Plunkett had stepped on the scale. Ewbank fumed.

"You weigh 337," the coach snapped. "I told you to report at no more than 300."

Plunkett argued mildly later that he had weighed 336, that "one pound makes a difference." But he soon was released. Walton had his job. On the first play of the season opener against the Chiefs at Kansas City, the rookie drove a forearm into Jerry Mays's neck. Mays was never a factor in that game. When it ended, Joe Namath congratulated the tackle.

"Sam," the quarterback said, "you did the best job on Mays that I've ever seen."

But two weeks later in Buffalo, the rookie was unable to handle the Bills' Ron McDole. Two weeks after that, Richie Jackson of the Denver Broncos pushed Walton around so often that Ewbank benched him. Against the Raiders in Oakland, he was benched again, as Ewbank switched Dave Herman from guard to tackle. When the Jets were preparing to oppose the Raiders in the AFL championship game, Herman again was at tackle. Herman did so well that Ewbank didn't dare risk Walton against the Colts.

Now, as the elevator door began to close, a stranger about 35, in a blue sports jacket, rushed up. With a drink in one hand, the stranger shoved his other hand against the door and it automatically reopened.

"Matt Snell?" the stranger asked, staring at Walton.

"No," the rookie replied.

"Willie Richardson?" he tried.

"No."

"Who?" said the stranger, his glass tilting.

"Emerson Boozer," said Walton, with a smile.

"Emerson, you're a great player," the stranger said, studying Walton's proportions. "How much do you go?"

"About 215."

The stranger sized up Walton's huge frame.

"You're a big 215. I'm 190, you go more than 215."

"That's all."

"What school? Florida A&M? Arizona State?"

"Maryland State," Walton answered quickly, giving Boozer's school.

"Good school, but you're more than 215. You sure you're in shape?"

"I'm a little bloated now," Walton said, "I had a big dinner."

"You must've had five dinners."

"I'll run it all off tomorrow."

"And you can really run, Emerson, you can really run. I've seen you run. Good luck, Emerson, good luck now."

The stranger wobbled away. The door finally closed. The elevator ascended. Harvey Nairn slapped his hands and burst out laughing. Sam Walton was laughing so hard, the elevator trembled.

Out by the pool, Joe Namath was talking to Larry Fox of the New York *Daily News.*

"Shula got pretty upset today," Fox said, "when the guys were asking him for his reaction to the way you rated Lamonica over Morrall. He didn't like anybody rapping his quarterback."

"Do me a favor," said Namath.

"What's that?"

"The next time you see Shula, tell him I wasn't rapping Morrall, that all I said was that I think Lamonica is a better quarterback. That's not rapping Morrall, that's the truth."

In darkness, except for the widening beam of light flashing the film on the wall, the projector whirred. Every so often, as he dissected the Baltimore Colt offense, Jet linebacker Larry Grantham would snap off the projector, reverse the film, then view the play again. On the other bed, Rocky Rochester, with a bottle of Schlitz in one hand, squinted now as he studied the flight of a long pass.

"Another balloon ball," Rochester said.

"He can't throw long," Grantham agreed.

They were watching Earl Morrall operate against the Minnesota Vikings in the NFL Western Conference title game, but they were not impressed.

"The long ones he does complete," Rochester said, "he needs a great catch, like that one by Richardson."

Larry Grantham sipped on a beer, too. When the Jets go into their defensive huddle, he calls their formation. Now, as the projector whirred in the hotel room, his deep-set eyes searched for weaknesses in the Colt offense and checked Morrall's tendencies as a play-caller.

"He likes to go to Mackey over the middle," Rochester said.

"He should," Grantham said. "Mackey is the best he's got."

"Hudson's got to play him tight."

"He will, and a linebacker will be with him. We're going to gamble on double-covering with a linebacker. We can't let Mackey break loose."

"Short ones, but no long ones."

Grantham nodded. Sharp featured, with a big dimple in his chin and with tight blond curly hair, he was selected in 1960 by the Colts as well as the New York Titans. At the University of Mississippi, he had been known primarily as an offensive end. But he realized that he had been drafted for his potential as a linebacker. At the time the Colts had won two consecutive NFL championships and their linebackers were well established.

"The offers were the same," Grantham has said, "but I knew I'd play more in New York."

He did, but he played with a stigma. "Too light for the NFL," the critics gossiped. He weighed around 200 pounds, and a linebacker *had* to weigh more than that. His weight was listed in programs at as much as 207, but that was exaggerated.

"I don't think I've ever been higher than 205 when I play," he confessed in 1965, "and by the end of the season, I'm usually down to around 192."

He had added some weight since then, but he remained the lightest starting linebacker in either league. The accepted *minimum* weight for a linebacker had become 220, and many of them were 235 and 240. But Grantham had continued to excel even though the average size of opposing players he was primarily responsible for tackling—the running backs and the tight ends—had grown bigger each year.

"If you were coming out of college now," Walt Michaels once kidded him, "we'd say you were too small."

"I'd have to agree with that," Grantham replied. "I'm just glad that I'm here already, so nobody will notice."

As the right linebacker, he depended on quickness and sure-handed tackling to compensate for his lightness. His knowledge of defensive formations had increased his value, but the weight factor had haunted him. Not that Larry Grantham hadn't put on a few pounds. According to the Super Bowl publicity, he had filled out to 212 pounds. But now, during a change of film in the darkened room, Rocky Rochester glanced at him.

"What did you weigh at practice today?" Rocky asked.

"Two hundred and two. But don't you dare tell anybody."

"I won't," Rocky said, "but have another beer."

TUESDAY, JANUARY 7

"We're Going to Have Poise and Execution"

For the first time, the sun was out in the morning, and at breakfast, Dave Herman was peering through his horned-rim glasses at *The Wall Street Journal*.

"IBM lost nine-and-a-half points," he was saying to Frank Ramos, the Jets' public-relations director. "The biggest single drop of the day. Another civil anti-trust suit was filed against it. Bad news like that will do that every time."

Herman, whose task would be to block Bubba Smith, is also employed by T. L. Watson & Company, a Wall Street firm.

"The general market had its worst day in nearly a year and a half," he said, "imagine that, *a year and a half.*"

"And on Sunday," said Ramos, grinning, "Bubba Smith will have his worst day in nearly a year and a half."

Herman pretended to have not heard the remark, but his forehead betrayed his awareness. In the middle of that forehead is a bump about the size of a quarter—a calcium deposit that developed over the years from blocking with his helmet. Now, as he studied the stock market tables, that bump was protruding slightly more than usual. Of all the Jets, he had perhaps the single most difficult assignment. Not only did he have the responsibility of preventing Bubba Smith, the ogre of the Colts, from assaulting Joe Namath, but he had to do it from a strange position and on a damaged ankle.

Throughout his Jet career, he had been a guard. Suddenly, he now was a tackle.

"The switch is much different than most people think," he had said a few days earlier. "At tackle, you're blocking a defensive end, and he lines up outside you. When you're a guard, the other team's tackle lines up on your head. The end comes at you from a different angle, and that means you have to adjust your blocking technique. I know the assignments. And if you know what you're to do, and if you execute properly, you should be able to do it. But you've got to make sure that you *do* it. One breakdown and you could get your quarterback hurt."

His transfer to tackle had occurred two weeks earlier, although it had been tested during the season.

In the regular-season game at Oakland, rookie tackle Sam Walton was being overpowered by Ike Lassiter, and he was benched. In the emergency, Weeb Ewbank moved Herman from right guard to right tackle. The strategy succeeded. Herman controlled Lassiter. But for the remaining four games of the schedule, Walton started. Herman, meanwhile, incurred a bruised right ankle in the next-to-last regular-season game, and he played only briefly until the AFL championship contest.

But for that game, Ewbank did not dare risk Walton against Lassiter, and the coach designated Herman as the starting tackle. Randy Rasmussen, who had alternated at left guard with Bob Talamini, was inserted at right guard.

Herman blocked Lassiter almost flawlessly, a vital factor in the Jets' triumph. "Beginner's luck," he would joke later. But his performance qualified him for the Super Bowl's most publicized pairing: the transplanted tackle against big Bubba, the 6-foot 7-inch, 295-pound defensive end who had inspired the chant, "Kill, Bubba, Kill" during his senior year at Michigan State. To add to the drama of the matchup, Herman was a senior at State when Bubba was a freshman.

"But our only contact with the freshmen was social," Herman had said. "We didn't scrimmage the freshmen."

In college, Herman had acquired a nickname of his own—Haystack. It was borrowed from the barefoot wrestler Haystack Calhoun, whose weight was advertised as 601 pounds. He knew about haystacks. He had grown up on his family's farm in Edon, Ohio, where the population was 750, and he had been an impressive lineman in high school. But his little high school could not afford the expense of taking films of its games. As a result, when he sought a college scholarship, there was nothing to show college coaches.

"But the guy who sold us feed for our poultry," he recalled, "knew a guy who knew a guy at Michigan State."

He received a scholarship and made the most of it. During his senior season, he was drafted by both the Jets and the New York Giants. He chose the Jets because George Sauer, Sr., the player personnel director, was more determined to sign him than the Giants' representative had been. He soon developed into one of the AFL's finest guards.

But Ewbank noticed a deficiency.

"Why," the coach asked him early in the 1968 season, "are you always moving your head around out there?"

"I have trouble seeing," Herman explained. "My eyes are 20/200 to 20/300, and I'm color blind."

Color blindness didn't affect his play because the opposing team wears either dark jerseys or white jerseys. Off the field, he wore his horned-rim glasses to correct his astigmatism. Although the astigmatism didn't detract from his pass-blocking or his straight-ahead blocking, it had been a factor when he pulled out of the line to lead a sweep play and he had to decide instantaneously whether to go inside or outside of the tight end.

"Sometimes I'd go outside," he confessed, "and it would mess things up."

Ewbank ordered contact lenses, which had to be made to fit the irregular curvature of Herman's eyeballs.

"Now he'll see what he's doing," the coach said, "instead of feeling his way."

"Weeb thinks," Herman said, "a little pair of contacts will make me a superman."

In the AFL championship game, he had been a superman. But in his matchup with big Bubba, he would have to be a superman again. Now, as he folded *The Wall Street Journal* after breakfast, Frank Ramos offered him a batch of Fort Lauderdale, Miami, and New York newspapers.

"No thanks," Dave Herman said. "The only paper I'm reading this week is *The Wall Street Journal*. No sports section."

Dave Herman hadn't remembered much about Bubba Smith when they were at Michigan State, but big Bubba remembered.

"It wasn't the way he said," Bubba later recalled. "We did too scrimmage the varsity, and I can remember him hollering at the guys on the freshman team. I can't stand people to holler at me, and he was always sort of mean to us younger players."

The gray metallic movie projectors were empty. The white screens had been rolled up. The game films remained in their round, gray metal cans.

No movies would be shown today because the Jets' coaches were about to disclose "The Game Plan." The entire meeting would be devoted to it. Each of the players had been issued a blue folder, the Colts' color, with a blank label where each would write "Super Bowl" and his name. Inside, on the title page, they were reminded that the Colt record was "15 Wins, 1 Loss" and they were exhorted that "A Great Effort with Dedication Can Win Everything."

At one end of the Imperial Room, where the members of the offensive unit had assembled, offensive coach Clive Rush presided.

"All receivers," Rush was saying now, "should read, react, and adjust to their multiple coverage. And receivers and the quarterback should *think* safety blitz as you approach the line, remember to *think* safety blitz, they use it a lot."

The Colts liked to use a safetyman to blitz the opposing quarterback, but that exposed an uncovered area.

"When that safetyman blitzes," Rush continued, "the outside receivers should react with a slant pattern."

Rush was reading from two pages of single-spaced typewritten instructions prepared for the coaches and the quarterbacks. The other offensive players—the backs, the receivers, and the linemen—were not burdened with these overall instructions. They were expected to make notes on whatever pertained to their particular individual responsibility.

One by one, Rush, with the analytical manner of a physics professor, went through the mimeographed pages of the offensive plan.

Clive Rush, Joe Spencer, and Weeb Ewbank had looked at Colt films for about thirty hours, developing "square eyeballs," as Spencer liked to joke. But their observations had been condensed into seven pages of information.

On the first page was a basic list of Colt defensive personnel, names and numbers.

On the second page was the list of plays that, the coaches believed, would work best against the Colt defense. Three formations were to be used—flank, split, and slot. From the flank formation, there were six runs, four passes, and four play-passes (meaning passes which are disguised as runs). From the split formation, there were five runs, seven passes, and four play-passes. From the slot formation, there were five runs, seven passes, and four play-passes.

On the third page were diagrams of the Colts' six primary defenses.

On the fourth page were diagrams of the Colts' six stunting defenses.

The fifth, sixth, and last pages were devoted to diagrams of Colt blitzes.

"When option blocking and running," Rush was saying now, "sustain on your man the way he wants to go, and our back will break for daylight."

Across the room, the defensive unit was listening to Walt Michaels, his brawny arms emphasizing his words.

"Their offensive line," Michaels was saying, "is about like Kansas City, and we handled Kansas City's offense. We held them without a touchdown."

Michaels, Buddy Ryan, and Ewbank needed twenty-five pages to diagram all the Colt plays they had observed.

"From their flank formation," Michaels was saying, "they use our 34 power, our 35 power, our slant 14, slant 15, our 18 straight and our 19 straight, our 10 straight, our 25 lag and our 24 lag. From their split, they use our 34 and 35 power, 34 and 35 trap, 36 and 37 power."

Michaels then dissected the Colt plays from their slot, double-wing, flood and power-"I" formations.

"And safetymen," he was saying now, an urgency in his voice, "always be aware of Mackey, be ready for Mackey on the reverse and the screen. Matte will throw a halfback running pass, and he will also throw back to Morrall for our 438 throwback play."

Throughout the meeting, a short, sharp-faced, white-haired man in green slacks and a green sweater had been a guest.

Phil Iselin, a modest millionaire who made his money in the women's-wear business, had been elevated to the presidency of the Jets the previous summer, following the death of Don Lillis, who had organized the purchase of Sonny Werblin's stock. Iselin, also the president of the Monmouth Park racetrack in New Jersey, was a member of the Werblin-led group that reorganized the New York franchise in 1963. The other members of that group were Townsend Martin, a millionaire sportsman and now the club's chairman of the board, and Leon Hess, the oil-company president and the wealthiest of the owners. Lillis's stock had been inherited by Mrs. Helen Springborn, the club's lady vice-president.

But now, for the first time, Phil Iselin was sitting in on the game-plan meeting that Weeb Ewbank was about to conclude.

"All right, now," Ewbank said. "We don't want to be fancy. We want to be fundamental, to be sound. We want two things—to be in better physical shape than they are, and to study more.

"And the most important thing is to retain your poise. We don't want to have happen to us what happened to the AFL teams in the other Super Bowl games. Two years ago, Len Dawson was intercepted early in the second half to set up a Packer touchdown, and he let that upset him. Last year, Rodger Bird fumbled a punt, then the Raiders had a miscoverage on defense, and the Packers got a field goal that put them in command right before halftime."

The interception of Dawson's pass led to a 21–10 deficit for the Chiefs. Bird's fumble dropped the Raiders behind, 16–7.

"We hope that nothing like that happens to us," Ewbank continued, "but if it does, we're not going to let it upset us. We're going to have poise and execution. *Poise and execution.* If they get a touchdown, we'll come back with two. If we need 50 points to win, we expect to get them from our offense. And if we need a shutout to win, we expect to get that from our defense. Whatever it takes to win, we expect to get it.

"All right now, execute this game plan with the same pride and authority that made us the champions of the AFL and we will be the champions of the world."

With a whoop, all the players arose, their blue folders in hand, and filed through the adjoining Bimini Room toward the buses that would take them to practice. Ewbank, leaning on his cane, was hobbling after them when Iselin approached him.

"I really enjoyed that, Weeb," the club president said. "I never realized how involved a game plan is."

"It does get involved," Ewbank agreed. "We don't just throw the ball up and listen for the thud."

With his chiseled profile, gleaming teeth and dark-blond wavy hair, Mike Curtis looks, says artist LeRoy Neiman, "like Hugh O'Brian would like to look."

"I am a gentleman off the field," the Colt linebacker said, "and an animal on the field."

And so his nickname, "The Animal," developed. He appeared to enjoy the notoriety of it.

"I play football," he also had said, "because it's the only way you can hit people and get away with it."

He had a reputation for hitting hard, even in a routine practice session. Several weeks earlier, he had been fooled on a play by Tom Matte. On the next play, in angry embarrassment, Curtis chased down Terry Cole, another Colt back, and tackled him so hard that Coach Don Shula ordered him to the sidelines to cool off.

"It's a good thing Shula didn't say much," Curtis said at the time, "or I might have slugged him."

And now, he was explaining his boyhood aggressions to John Crittendon of the *Miami News*.

"The other kids liked to throw snowballs," he said, "but I liked to throw rocks. My idea of a good time was a BB gun fight. I didn't just like to ride a bicycle—that was too tame. I like to ride my bicycle into something."

On Sunday, he would have his opportunity to run his bicycle into Joe Namath.

Snow decorated the bleak hills surrounding Beaver Falls, Pennsylvania, about 30 miles northwest of Pittsburgh.

In the number two hot mill of the Babcock & Wilcox Company, 61-year-old John Namath was measuring a white-hot strip of steel. In the summer, the temperature in his section of the mill rises to about 120 degrees. In the winter, it drops to about 80. "You have to wear thermal underwear all the time," he says, "to keep the heat off your body." Above him, big fans hum constantly. This has been his life. He has been a member of the United Steelworkers since 1936, and he was working in this mill for three years before his fourth son, Joseph William, was born on May 31, 1943.

"When are you leaving for the game?" somebody asked.

"Friday morning," he said, "and I'll be back Monday."

"Too bad you're going to make that trip for nothing."

"You'll see," he said. "There are four AFL teams that could beat the Colts. You'll see."

"Not the Colts."

He would miss four days' pay, but he had occasionally missed a day or two in order to see his son play. During the season, he had seen him in New York in a 26–7 victory over the Houston Oilers, and he had seen him in Buffalo in that travesty of five interceptions, three of which were run back for touchdowns as the Bills won an upset, 37–35. After that loss, he had watched his son hobble out of the shower.

"How's the knee?"

"Dad, it hurts."

The quarterback's right knee was damaged initially in 1964, but this was the first time he had acknowledged to his father that pain existed in it. When the quarterback was dressed, he limped toward the steep flight of wooden steps that leads to the War Memorial Stadium's street level. Awkwardly, painfully, he gripped the railing during his slow descent.

"Look at him," his father whispered to a bystander. "He can hardly walk."

Seeing him like this, his father remembered a telephone call the previous Christmas.

"Joe phoned," his father said, "and he told me that he hadn't gotten me a present yet, and he wanted to know if there was anything special I'd like. I told him, 'I would be the happiest man in the world if you gave me one thing.' He asked me what it was, and I told him, 'If you stopped playing football.' He said, 'You don't mean that,' and I said, 'I guess I don't.'"

"But," the bystander said, "did you mean it?"

"I did," John Namath said. "I certainly did."

On the bus to practice, George Sauer, Jr., turned to Johnny Sample.

"Have you read some of that stuff in the newspapers down here about us?"

"George," said Sample, "I haven't read a paper all week, and I won't."

In the locker room at Fort Lauderdale Stadium, several sportswriters surrounded Joe Namath as he slipped into a padded rib protector with sewn-in plastic slats.

"What's that?" one of them asked.

"It absorbs some of the shock when you get hit," the quarterback said. "It cuts down the jolt."

"Does it impede you?"

"No, I can still throw free."

"I meant your running."

"It does make me step slower," he said, smiling, "but it doesn't matter. Not a man with my speed."

Frank Ramos approached.

"The cameramen outside want you to put on your uniform jersey," the publicity man said.

"No," the quarterback said.

"It would look better on TV," Ramos said.

"Matt, you wearing a jersey?"

At his nearby locker, Matt Snell glared.

"I paid $50 not to wear one," he replied.

Ramos backed off, and the sportswriters resumed chatting with the quarterback.

"Did you see the piece I did on you in the Sunday paper?" one of them asked him.

"I haven't been getting the papers. By the time I get downstairs, they're gone."

"By the time you get downstairs," said Babe Parilli, "the next day's are on sale."

In the recovery room at College Hospital, Jimmy "The Greek" Snyder was awake after surgery. Above him the doctor was explaining the situation.

"We got that thing out," he said, "but we have to send it to be analyzed just in case, you know."

"Yeah, I know. In case it's cancer."

"Don't worry," the doctor said. "I doubt that it is. I doubt it so much I'll give you 100 to 1."

Jimmy smiled.

"I'll take it."

Randy Beverly was sitting on the gray locker-room bench, tying the laces of his football shoes before practice. Somewhat short at 5 feet, 11 inches, but with a powerful torso and sturdy thighs on his 198-pound body, he pretends to exist in the utmost of cool, and the approaching Super Bowl had not changed him.

"I've never seen Jimmy Orr," he was saying. "I don't even know how tall he is."

As the right cornerback, Beverly would cover Orr, the Colts' experienced split end.

"How big is Orr?" he said, turning to Johnny Sample. "I've never seen him."

"He's your height, maybe a bit smaller," Sample said. "But you've never seen him?"

"Never," said Beverly, softly. "How would I see him? I never was in the NFL."

"Not even on television?" Sample asked.

"I saw him on television a couple of years ago, but I don't count that. You don't really see a man on television. Even in the movies, that's not really *seeing* him."

"I can't believe that," Sample said.

Randy Beverly shrugged, unperturbed, and continued to tie his shoelaces. He had been tying them for many years without too much recognition. He grew up in Wildwood, New Jersey, near Atlantic City. He was an all-state schoolboy in football and track. He went to Trinidad Junior College in Colorado, where he helped the team win a national junior college football championship. He transferred to Colorado State University, where he starred as an offensive halfback as well as at several other positions, but he was not drafted by any of the professional teams. As a free agent, he later was contacted by a few.

"San Diego, Denver, and Houston in the AFL got in touch with me," he has said, "and so did the Canadian teams, but nobody in the NFL talked to me. I picked the Jets because they were closer to home."

His first season, 1966, he played with a team even closer to home—the Jersey City Jets of the Atlantic Coast Football League, a Jets' minor-league affiliate. He also was a member of the Jet taxi-squad, that group of reservists who practice with the members of the forty-man roster but do not dress for Sunday games. Not that he was forgotten by the team. His speed had impressed Walt Michaels, the assistant coach.

"Beverly," said Michaels that season, "runs the 40 in 4.5, and you can't get speed like that. We're not giving up on him."

The next season, 1967, that speed began to show. After surviving the training-camp cuts, Beverly was inserted at cornerback late in the first half of an early season game at Denver when the Jets fell behind by 17 points. He and the other defenders held the Broncos scoreless while Joe Namath rallied the offense to victory.

Ever since, Randy Beverly has been the right cornerback. And a quietly aggressive one. On the next-to-last play of the Jets' 37–35 loss in Buffalo during the 1968 season, Beverly knocked Haven Moses unconscious. Moses, a rookie, was flanked to the left, close to the sideline and in front of the Jet bench. At the snap, as Moses was looking in toward his quarterback, Beverly flattened him with a forearm chop.

Moses lay still for about thirty seconds, then had to be helped to his feet. He wobbled to the bench.

Although no penalty was called, perhaps because the flow of the play was to the other side of the field, a routine review of the game films at the Commissioner's headquarters in New York resulted in Beverly being fined $100 by Pete Rozelle. But Beverly maintained his cool. "I just bumped him," he told a newsman. "*Bumped?*" the newsman said. "You might as well have hit him with an ax."

"That's what we call bumping," he said. That's what the Commissioner's office called unnecessary roughness, subject to fine. Now, in the days before the Super Bowl game, he had forgotten the Moses incident. His responsibility now was to cover Jimmy Orr. The split end, small but slick, was completing his eleventh season in the NFL. He ranked fifth among its active players in receptions, with 365 for 7,241 yards and 62 touchdowns. He also ranked as a con man.

"He'll talk to you," Johnny Sample was saying now. "He'll try to lull you."

Sample had covered Orr when they were rivals in the NFL for many seasons.

"He'll line up the first time," Sample continued, "and he'll say, 'How you doing, nice weather we got, and now don't you hit me and I won't hit you.' One time I remember I hit him on the sideline and really bounced him along the ground. It was hard, maybe frozen, I've forgot, but when he got up, he told me, 'It's too cold to hit like that.' He's a cute one."

"But what does he do?" Beverly asked.

"He's got great hands, great moves."

"But a receiver can only do so many things," Randy Beverly said, with the utmost of cool. "Some guys just do them better than others."

Out on the field, Bill Mathis winked at a few Jet teammates and strolled near John Dockery.

"Ivy League practice," Mathis said loudly. "No pads, no hitting, Ivy League practice."

Dockery smiled. He was accustomed to the joking abuse. A graduate of Harvard, he was the only member of the Jets from an Ivy League college. Traditionally, players from the other major conferences, such as the Southeastern or the Big Ten, consider Ivy League products inferior. Perhaps with justification because there are only a handful of Ivy Leaguers in the NFL and AFL. But Dockery wasn't surrendering in silence.

"You guys need a little Ivy League class to polish up the Super Bowl," he told Mathis.

Slender, at 6 feet and 185 pounds, with black curly hair and a friendly face, John Dockery had been cut by the Jets at training camp in 1968. Although remaining on the taxi squad, he was dispatched to the Bridgeport, Connecticut, farm team in the Atlantic Coast Football League, and he spent the season there. But with three games remaining on the Jet schedule, Weeb Ewbank phoned his Brooklyn home.

"We're going to activate you," the coach said. "We need some help covering kicks."

In the previous game "Speedy" Duncan of the Chargers had returned a punt 95 yards for a touchdown. The Jets won, 37–15, but Ewbank was thinking ahead to the AFL championship game and to the Super Bowl—when a miscoverage on a punt-return could turn a game around. Quick and tough, Dockery would improve the punting and kickoff units, and suddenly, he was eligible for a $15,000 bonanza.

"All this week," he would say, "I kept thinking of that line from The Fantasticks'—you have to die a little to be born again."

And now, on the field at Fort Lauderdale Stadium, John Dockery, the Harvard man, dashed under a pass thrown by Jim Turner in the Tuesday practice known as "pat and go." When the passer pats the ball (instead of taking a snap from center), the receiver goes. No pads, no hitting.

Near the dugout, Joe Namath was finishing his final television interview of the afternoon. His arms were folded across his red practice jersey. His lips were pressed together, and his head was bobbing slightly, almost challengingly, as if he were daring Jack Perkins, the NBC newscaster, to ask a question that he couldn't answer glibly.

"Your team," intoned Perkins, "is an 18-point underdog. What about that?"

"I don't know anything about betting and odds and things like that," said the quarterback, "but that's a pretty big price."

Perkins ended the interview. They shook hands, and Namath strolled away.

Not far away, Matt Snell and Emerson Boozer ran easily in practice. They had been ignored by all the television crews and all the newspaper photographers.

Out on the beach, several of the wives were stretched out, sunning themselves.

"I feel guilty," Dotty Hampton, the wife of the equipment manager, said. "Our husbands are working, and we're loafing. We ought to be doing something."

"Ping-Pong," said Marilyn Maynard. "Let's go up and use the Ping-Pong table."

But soon after she began playing with Betsy Baker, she leaned across the table, reaching for the ball, and the table collapsed. "An omen," one of the wives said, content to relax.

"No," said Dotty, "let's play volleyball. The net is up. All we need is the ball. And we need the exercise." And so the volleyball games began among the wives.

No pads and no hitting had been the order of the day, but throughout practice, George Sauer, Jr., had worn both his helmet and shoulder pads.

"I don't want to turn too late on a pass and get a broken nose, and you have to be used to looking for the ball over the facebar," he was saying now at his locker. "And I don't want to run into somebody and pop a shoulder. I guess I read too much about Raymond Berry when I was a kid. He did all these things."

Weeb Ewbank had Raymond Berry when he was coaching the Colts.

"George Sauer," the coach often says, "is a *fast* Raymond Berry."

Don Maynard was in the whirlpool, soaking his left thigh, when he noticed Joe Namath talking to a sportswriter.

"Joe's really somethin'," the flanker said, chuckling. "When the charter got here the other night, he was on television when he got off, and the announcer said somethin' to him about having good receivers, and he said, '*Good*, is that all you can say about them, that they're just *good?* I have the *greatest* receivers in football.'"

Maynard laughed. "Joe's really somethin'," he said.

Out near the pool, Bake Turner was stretched out on a chaise longue. Nearby, a middle-aged woman in a silly straw hat stopped and stared at him.

"You one of the football players?" she asked.

"Yes, ma'am," the Texan said politely.

"Please explain something to me," she said. "Why is it all you players have such different shaped legs? Your legs are nice and slim, but some of the others are big and strong. Why is there such a difference?"

"That's because some of us are runners, ma'am, and some of us are hitters. I'm one of the runners."

One of the least appreciated Jets, too. He's better known for playing the guitar on the *Ed Sullivan Show*, the *Tonight Show*, and night-club stands than he is for playing football. On another team, he might be an outstanding pass-receiver. On the Jets, he has been shunted to the sideline by Don Maynard and George Sauer, Jr. But in the season finale, when Maynard rested his ailing thigh muscle, Turner caught 7 passes for 157 yards and was rewarded with the game ball. In two seasons before Sauer arrived, Turner caught 71 passes for 1,007 yards and 58 for 974 yards.

"He gives us depth at both wide-receiver spots," Weeb Ewbank likes to say, "and depth gives you a championship."

Robert Hardy Turner is a 28-year-old bachelor who got his nickname growing up in Alpine, in west Texas.

"I'm told," he says, "that when I was a kid, I always had a bacon rind in my mouth, so people started calling me Bacon Rind, then Bacon, then just Bake. I like it better than Bobby, but my mother still calls me that."

After a standout college career at Texas Tech, he joined the Colts in 1962 as their twelfth-round draft choice.

"Weeb used me on kickoff returns and punt returns that year," he recalls, "but the next year, I was gone."

So was Weeb, but when Don Shula realized that Willie Richardson, a Colt rookie in 1963, would eliminate Turner, he alerted Ewbank that the 180-pound Texan would be available. After signing with the Jets, he was voted their Most Valuable Player that year, but when young Sauer moved in, he virtually vanished. Understandably, he has asked to be traded.

"Don't worry," Ewbank would tell him, "I'll get you in there."

But nothing happened. To recreate his identity, he was one of the Jets who several weeks earlier had grown mustaches and goatees. He had shaved his mustache off after the clinching of the divisional title, but now he had regrown it—a thin, soft brown mustache that appeared to fascinate the middle-aged woman in the silly straw hat as much as his slim legs.

"Why do you have that mustache?" she said.

"I feel cockier with it, ma'am," he said.

Throughout the week, Gerry Philbin had been thinking about Sam Ball, the Colt offensive tackle whom he would be matched against. Now, as he finished dinner in a nearby restaurant, he noticed a 6-foot 4-inch, 250-pounder across the room and immediately recognized Ball.

"There he is," the defensive end growled to a companion. "I'm going to whip his ass."

In the dining room shortly before ten o'clock, Curley Johnson and Pete Lammons were finishing slabs of roast beef when Babe Parilli stopped by their table.

"Mike Holovak got fired today," Parilli said.

Holovak had coached the Boston Patriots of the AFL since early in the 1961 season. During his regime, his best player had been Vito Parilli, the "Sweet Kentucky Babe." In 1963, the quarterback had guided the Patriots to their only Eastern Division title. But in trying to rebuild the Patriots for the 1968 season, Holovak traded the 38-year-old Parilli to the Jets for Mike Taliaferro, another quarterback, in July. When the Patriots lost seven of their last eight games for a 4–10 record, Holovak was out. But the Babe had prospered, maintaining his successful image.

"You may be offered that job in Boston, dahlin'," Curley Johnson said.

"I don't want that job in Boston, dahlin'," Parilli replied seriously.

At his age, he had the practically perfect job. At the time of the trade, he had said, "I guess I'm supposed to be number two behind Joe, but I don't think I'm ready to be put aside just yet." He may have been number two behind Namath, but he showed his new teammates that he could produce when he had to, notably when the Jets were threatened with the embarrassment of defeat in their first game after clinching the divisional title. Weeb Ewbank had decided to use Namath in the first half of each of the remaining games and, no matter what the situation, to prepare Parilli for emergency duty in the championship game by playing him throughout the second half.

Early in the final quarter against the Miami Dolphins, the Jets were trailing by a field goal. During the third quarter, Parilli had not been able to guide the offense beyond the Dolphin 44-yard line.

But suddenly, Parilli completed two touchdown passes to Don Maynard within forty-two seconds. He added a third touchdown pass on a juggling catch by Bake Turner to assure a 35–17 victory. During the last three games of the regular season, he completed 26 of 48 passes for 367 yards and five touchdowns, remarkable statistics considering that his playing time amounted to only a game and a half. But his most important contribution to the Jets was as a ball-holder for place-kicker Jim Turner.

During his seasons with the Patriots, he had spotted the ball for Gino Cappelletti, who holds the AFL record for career field goals.

When Parilli joined the Jets, he immediately was assigned as Turner's holder. During one of their first practices, he made a suggestion.

"I know you've been spotting the ball at 7 yards," Parilli said, "but I'd like to move it up a few inches. That way, the ball should be coming into my hands with the laces facing the goalposts and I won't have to waste time spinning the ball to get the laces around facing them."

Turner agreed, and on center John Schmitt's next snap, Parilli placed the ball quickly. Turner booted it true.

"Babe, you've got the fastest hands I've ever seen," Turner said. "Any way you say is fine with me."

In addition to providing mechanical perfection as a ball-holder, Parilli increased Turner's confidence. His quiet, dignified personality also endeared him to his new teammates, almost all of whom were in grade school when he broke into pro football in 1952. Namath was 9 years old then, and he connects Parilli with the display window of the Army-Navy store in Beaver Falls, Pennsylvania.

"They had helmets with his name on them," Namath says. "He was from a town close by, Rochester."

Bart Starr, the Packer quarterback, considered enrolling at the University of Kentucky while Parilli was there.

"He showed me around the campus," Starr says. "He was my hero. I had his picture on my bedroom wall."

Parilli has endurance. When he was voted the "Most Valuable Player" in the 1952 College All-Star Game, his teammates included Frank Gifford, Gino Marchetti, Ollie Matson, Hugh McElhenny, and Bill Howton. The other quarterbacks were Billy Wade and Al Dorow. But Babe is the only member of that squad still active.

After two seasons with the Packers, he was traded to the Cleveland Browns in 1954. He spent the next two years in military service. Upon his return in 1956, he had an opportunity to replace the retired Otto Graham, but he was hindered by a shoulder injury.

"I only played in five games that season," he once complained. "I didn't get much of a chance."

Paul Brown, the coach of the Browns, returned him to the Packers, but in 1959, he was released by Coach Vince Lombardi, then in his first month of shaping the Packers into a dynasty.

"He never gave me a real reason for cutting me. I guess I simply represented the past."

Parilli moved to the Ottawa Rough Riders of the Canadian Football League, and when the AFL began operations in 1960, he joined the Oakland Raiders. The next year he was traded to the Patriots where he alternated at quarterback with Ed "Butch" Songin until Songin was injured. In 1963, many Fenway Park customers shouted for Mike Holovak to use Tom Yewcic at quarterback, but the coach preferred Parilli. Babe led the Patriots to their only

Eastern title. But even in triumph there was frustration. The Patriots lost the AFL championship game to the San Diego Chargers, 51–10.

Through it all, he seemed to be searching for the stature that would erase his stigma as an NFL reject.

"He's a shy, sensitive guy," remembers Blanton Collier, now the head coach of the Cleveland Browns, "and he had the finest arm I've ever seen on a boy coming out of college. To this day, I firmly believe that if Paul Brown had been more patient at Cleveland the Babe would have been one of the great quarterbacks in the NFL."

Nobody will ever know about that, but a decade after being cut by the Packers, Vito Parilli was about to oppose an NFL team again.

"Hey, where you goin'?" Curley Johnson was saying to him now in the dining room. "We got an hour until curfew, dahlin'. Time for a beer or two."

"No, thanks," the Babe replied. "I've got some reading to do."

He hurried off, through the Bimini Room toward the far elevator.

"If I know Babe," said Curley, "the only thing he'll be reading is the game plan."

Upstairs, in the Governor's Suite, the married member of its odd couple was on the phone with his wife.

"Now don't forget," Jim Hudson was saying to her, "bring those red shorts you gave me before the Orange Bowl game a few years ago. Don't forget now."

Shortly after their marriage, Wendy had purchased the shorts prior to Texas's triumph over Alabama.

"I won't forget," she assured him before hanging up. "I'll put them in my suitcase so I can't forget."

WEDNESDAY, JANUARY 8
"Seeing Him Might Scare Me Out"

Don Shula was up early, the bright sun slashing through the windows of his ocean-front room at the Statler Hilton. When he glanced down at the beach, he noticed his right cornerback, Lenny Lyles, running along the wet sand.

Lyles had been weakened by an attack of tonsilitis. His temperature had been 102 degrees the day before.

Seeing him, Shula was encouraged. He knew Lyles would have to be healthy to cover George Sauer, Jr.

Bob Talamini was in a hurry. At other times he had been relaxed and casual, although surrounded by his wife Charlene and the organized chaos of their four small children—5-year-old Robin Marie, 3-year-old Bobby, 2-year-old Tina Marie, and 1-year-old Tony. But now the black-haired, deep-chested left guard appeared concerned as he moved quickly between the people in the Galt lobby.

"What's the big rush?" somebody asked him.

"We've got a crisis upstairs," he replied.

"Is any of the kids sick?"

"No, we're out of Pampers."

He was talking about disposable diapers, and several minutes later he returned with three big boxes of them.

"I hope I'm in time," he said.

Despite the crisis, he was enjoying his family. Some players didn't want their wives and children around, thinking it might distract them, but not Bob Talamini. Throughout the season, his family had remained at their home in Houston. He had flown there to visit them a few times, but basically, he had led a bachelor's existence, sharing a room with Babe Parilli in the Sheraton-Tenney near Shea Stadium.

He had joined the Jets during training camp as the result of a trade with the Houston Oilers for a third-round draft choice.

"One of the best trades I think I ever made," Weeb Ewbank would say. "He's a real old pro, he does the job."

Talamini was 29—but he didn't play as though he was that old. He had played with the Oilers for seven seasons, earning All-AFL recognition six times. His departure was unusual for a lineman of his stature, but he had openly resented some of the higher salaries being paid to unproven rookies. When the Oiler general manager, Don Klosterman, refused to consider Talamini's request for a bigger raise, an impasse developed.

"There are times," Talamini explained later, "when a man has to take a stand."

He retired. But the new Jet offensive line coach, Joe Spencer, who had tutored Talamini with the Oilers, alerted Ewbank to the possible availability of a blue-chip lineman. The trade followed. Suddenly the Jets had an All-AFL guard. The day he reported, he was welcomed by Verlon Biggs.

"Nice to have you here," Biggs said. "That means you won't be banging into me anymore."

Tough and powerful at 6-foot 1-inch tall and 255 pounds, Talamini had tortured opposing players. But Biggs's reaction was surprising because as a guard, Talamini seldom was involved in blocking Biggs, a defensive end. But in his haste to impress his new coaches and teammates, Talamini pulled a leg muscle. He struggled to crack the starting lineup. Mostly, he alternated with Randy Rasmussen. But in the championship game, when Rasmussen moved to right guard, Talamini had justified his All-AFL reputation. Now he was about to compete in the Super Bowl after eight seasons in the "other" league.

"My wife and I thought about leaving the kids home," he was saying now in the elevator, the diapers under his arm, "but we decided they deserved to be a part of all this—even if they do produce a crisis now and then."

No such crisis existed for Bill Rademacher, one of the outside men on the Jets' kickoff and punting units.

The sun had lured him out near the beach by ten o'clock, but as he played shuffleboard with Jim Richards, he thought about Timmy Brown, who would be running back kickoffs and punts for the Colts, and how he couldn't let Brown get around him to the sideline.

"Your shot," Richards reminded him.

"Oh, yeah," Rademacher said.

In the Rum House, Weeb Ewbank was holding his morning press conference.

"I'm not worried about the Colts' safety blitz," the coach was saying. "We picked up every safety blitz anybody threw at us this year. We didn't miss one. The season before, they tried four safety blitzes against us, and we only missed one. John is very good at reading the defense and picking up this sort of thing."

Confused, some of the newsmen glanced at each other.

"I mean Joe," said the coach who, apparently subconsciously, had transposed his most famous quarterbacks, Unitas and Namath.

Dozens of newsmen were milling about the Galt lobby, talking to various players. They were ignoring Mike D'Amato, and he was glad.

"If any of them had talked to me," he would say later, "I'm sure they would've brought up the 'Heidi' game. Whenever anybody asks me about that, my back stiffens up."

He had been the goat of the last-minute loss to the Raiders in Oakland. He had replaced Jim Hudson, following the strong-side safetyman's ejection in the third quarter. In the final minute, he missed a coverage on Charlie Smith, the Raiders' rookie halfback. Daryle Lamonica passed to Smith for a 43-yard touchdown that put the Raiders ahead to stay.

"It wasn't as if Smith had beaten me with a move," D'Amato, tall and handsome, says. "I made a mental mistake. I missed a defense. Inexperience. I had played well until that one play."

But that one play had haunted the 204-pound rookie from Hofstra University and now, as he strode through the lobby, he was hoping that none of the sportswriters would approach him for an interview. He didn't want to talk about the "Heidi" game, or think about it. Because if something happened to Hudson, he would have to cover John Mackey.

Joe Namath was up early—for him. "This curfew is killing me," the quarterback complained, grinning. "I'm getting too much sleep."

Billy Ray Smith, the Arkansas philosopher and defensive tackle of the Colts, was talking about Namath.

"That man can throw a football into a teacup at 50 yards," he said, "but he hasn't seen defenses like ours in the AFL. Our defenses are as complicated as some teams' offenses. We have twenty variations in our blitzes and five or six alignments up front. That lets us do a lot of things. I think reading our defenses will be a new experience for that man."

Although he was nearly 34 years old, Billy Ray Smith appeared rejuvenated by the Jet quarterback's presence. "He's a good quarterback," he said, "but he's a young man. When he gets a little older, he'll get humility."

Back at the Galt, the Jets were watching more films of the Colts during their meeting. When it ended, Pete Lammons passed Weeb Ewbank and winked at him.

"Coach," the tight end said, "you better stop showing us these films. We're getting overconfident."

Ewbank smiled. For the first time, he had the feeling that his players would not be awed by the Colts, and that perhaps Joe Namath's optimism had been contagious.

In the locker room at Fort Lauderdale Stadium, the Jets were surprised to see Bobby Sharp, their little 24-year-old assistant equipment manager, performing his chores.

"I didn't think you were coming," Clive Rush said to him.

"I didn't think so, either," Bobby replied, "but I got lucky."

The previous Thursday, when the players gathered at Shea Stadium before the chartered flight, he had been busy packing one of the trunks when Joe Namath noticed him.

"You making the trip?" the quarterback said.

"I got shut out," Bobby said. "I'm low man."

"You come down as soon as you can," Namath said, "and I'll pay your way."

Out on the beach at the Galt, the wives' volleyball game had begun. Perhaps the best player was Jackie Ramos, the public-relations director's wife. She had earned the nickname of "Slugger," but now tiny Freda Gordon entered the game for the first time.

"Here comes Black Power," she announced.

The others laughed, but not for long. Although weighing less than 100 pounds, she was one of the best volleyball players.

Before practice, Dave Herman had received an injection of Xylecaine to numb the pain in his battered right ankle. He would work strenuously today, and Dr. Jim Nicholas wanted him to become accustomed to laboring with a numbed ankle if he should require one on Sunday. But now he was being prepared for his confrontation with Bubba Smith, the ogre.

"All right," Buddy Ryan, the defensive line coach yelled, "next five plays, Philbin and Biggs switch sides."

Verlon Biggs, at 270 pounds, was the biggest man on the defensive unit and perhaps the most powerful. Ordinarily, he was the right end but the coaches wanted Herman to work not only against Philbin, who depends on quickness and agility, but also against Biggs, whose slam-bang style is more like big Bubba's.

"What do you want me to do?" Biggs asked Herman.

"Try to come over the top of me," Herman said, "and try to grab hold of me and throw me, like Bubba tries to do. But don't tell me which one you're going to do."

"Go to it, Flip," said Ryan, calling Biggs by his nickname.

In rushing a passer, Biggs likes to flip his forearm up into a blocker, knocking him off balance. He is powerful enough to do it. When he joined the Jets as a third-round draft choice out of Jackson State in Mississippi, he strolled into the trainer's room for his routine medical exam. Seeing the rookie's physique, Dr. Nicholas smiled.

"Do you lift weights?" the doctor said.

"Never have, Doc, never done anything like that."

"Then how did you build yourself up?"

"Just lived, that's all. Just lived."

But for three seasons, he lived as a man apart from most of his teammates. In the defensive huddle, he hardly spoke. Suddenly, in 1968, he emerged from his shell. At a critical point in an exhibition game, he startled the other members of the defensive unit.

"All right now," he growled, "let's hold 'em."

Mentioning it later, one of the defensive players said it was the first time he had heard Biggs talk in the huddle. Not long after that, Biggs was the one who suggested that the defensive linemen put $10 into their version of an office pool. The one who tackles the quarterback with the ball most often during a game collects the pot.

"When you get to the quarterback," Biggs likes to say, "you feel you've really accomplished something."

In the AFL championship game, Biggs *really* accomplished something. With the Jets leading, 27–23, in the closing minutes, the Raiders had a fourth down on the Jets' 26-yard line. Instead of attempting a field goal, they gambled on making a first down. But when Daryle Lamonica took the snap, he was flattened almost immediately.

Verlon Biggs had swooped in and grabbed the quarterback with the towering strength of a Kodiak bear.

Now, on the practice field in Fort Lauderdale, he was using that strength to impersonate big Bubba. As the ball was snapped, he yanked Dave Herman aside and crashed past him.

"Is that how he does it?" Biggs asked, seriously. "He better not," Herman snarled. "He better not."

On the sideline, Don Maynard picked up a football and tossed it to Dr. Nicholas.

"Throw me a few passes, Doc," he said. "I want to run a little to test my leg."

Loping at an easy jog, Maynard turned and caught the softly spiraled pass. But after he caught a few more, he shook his head and walked slowly to where Dr. Nicholas was standing.

"It's no good," the flanker said. "It feels like I might pull it. I can't run."

The offensive unit had another casualty. John Schmitt, the center, had twisted his left knee while running in yesterday's Ivy League practice. He had put on an old pair of shoes and the well-worn cleats had slipped on the grass. Schmitt, like Joe Namath, has had three knee operations, but as a member of what he calls "The Silent Service," his knee problems were virtually unpublicized.

Although he was elated by his players' attitude, Weeb Ewbank was worried about the absence of Maynard and Schmitt.

Throughout the practice, which concentrated on the offensive preparations for the Super Bowl game, the old coach moved around constantly, chatting with this player, suggesting something to that one, or confiding quietly with the other coaches.

Johnny Sample, wearing his weighted leather spats, noticed Ewbank's involvement with everything.

"Look at him," he told a teammate. "He usually concentrates on one thing, but not this week."

When the workout ended, most of the players disappeared through the dugout, but Joe Namath and George Sauer had remained on the field, Namath was slouched at an imaginary line of scrimmage and when he slapped the ball, Sauer would break downfield, then cut sharply toward the sideline in what is known as a square-out pattern. Behind him, Namath, having moved back quickly in his tiptoe style, would arrow the ball at him, precisely where Sauer could catch it and precisely where a cornerback could not.

After about a dozen such passes, Weeb Ewbank became impatient with his two perfectionists.

"That's enough," the coach said. "Don't leave all the good ones here. Save some for Sunday."

But before he departed, Namath, his torso sweating under his red jersey, sat on the grass and flopped backward. Suddenly, his torso snapped forward in a quick series of situp exercises.

"I do one hundred and fifty a day," he would say later. "I start out with seventy-five at training camp and increase it."

Not far away, the showers were hissing, the steam rising from the wet tile floor. But in the quiet of the trainer's room, Carl McAdams waited patiently. Dr. Nicholas had prepared two syringes of Depo-Medrol, a cortisone derivative—one for McAdams, the other for

Verlon Biggs, whose right ankle had been sore for several weeks. During his injection, Biggs remained as still as a stone statue and then strolled away without a word.

"Absolutely impassive," the doctor said. "I don't think I've ever seen anybody as impassive as that guy."

McAdams had developed a similar shell. The inside of his left ankle is scarred as if it had been seared by a misshaped branding iron. In the summer of 1966 he fractured the ankle in Chicago on a night out with some of his college All-Star teammates. His reputation as a linebacker at the University of Oklahoma had earned him a $350,000 contract from the Jets, but his ankle injury had made him useless. He needed three operations. One to set the ankle. Another when infected skin had to be replaced by a skin-graft from his thigh. And a third to remove the surgical pin in the ankle.

"I was in the hospital for thirteen weeks," he once said. "Seven in Chicago, six in New York."

When he was released, he needed crutches for several more weeks, then a cane. And he would hobble to Shea Stadium to sit in the whirlpool bath and exercise his ankle. When the season ended, he worked several hours a day to rebuild the muscles in his left leg. And all the time, he was eating heavily to regain the weight he had lost in the hospital.

"I weighed around 235 when I broke the ankle," he has said, "but when I got out of the hospital, I was down to 190. I was so upset emotionally, I couldn't eat."

The baby-faced rancher in Farris, Oklahoma, had the ideal size for a middle linebacker. But the injury had restricted his lateral movement, one of his many talents. When he finally was able to play, shortly after the 1967 season began, he was placed on the special teams, a dangerous assignment even for the soundest of players.

"I thought about letting him break in with Waterbury," said Weeb Ewbank, referring to the Jets' farm team that season in the Atlantic Coast Football League. "But if I'm going to get him hurt, I might as well get him hurt here."

During the 1968 season, McAdams was inserted at left tackle on the defensive unit as an occasional replacement for Rocky Rochester, particularly in an obvious passing situation by the opponents. In the 48–14 rout of the Boston Patriots, he recovered two fumbles that positioned the Jets for touchdowns. At last he had begun to contribute to the team, and he felt a part of its success.

"I could've gone back to my ranch and never played again," he has said, "but I didn't want anybody to call me a quitter."

Now, as the doctor completed the injection into his scarred ankle, Carl McAdams stood on it, limped momentarily and walked out toward his locker.

"That kid is in tears with pain after almost every game," the doctor said, "but he never whines about anything."

In the last bus returning from practice, a shout went up from several players: "John Free, let's stop for hot dogs. C'mon, John Free, tell the bussy to stop." Ahead was a red stand with a sign proclaiming "The World's Greatest Hot Dogs."

Soon about a dozen hungry players invaded the premises. When they had been served, Free began to chat with the counterman.

"You missed the world's greatest promotion," the traveling secretary said. "You should have had a camera to take a picture of this— a bus with a New York Jets sign outside, and all these players in here eating your hot dogs."

"Jets, schmets," said the counterman. "I had enough trouble keeping track of how many I sold."

Most of the players traveled to and from practice in the chartered buses, but a few used rented cars. Bill Mathis was driving a white convertible and among his passengers returning to the Galt were Joe Namath and Jim Hudson.

"How about some gin rummy tonight?" Mathis said.

"Forget it," Namath said. "I remember what happened in Oakland."

"We'll play your stakes," Mathis said.

"Forget it," Hudson said. "No chance."

When the Jets were in Oakland for the regular-season game, Mathis and Babe Parilli, who had a running gin-rummy game all season, accepted a challenge from Namath and Hudson for a four-handed game. Namath suggested stakes of ten cents a point, ten dollars a game, and two dollars and fifty cents a box, but Mathis and Parilli considered that to be too expensive. Eventually they agreed on two cents a point, one dollar a game, and fifty cents a box.

"And we cleaned 'em out," Mathis would say later, "for about $200 apiece."

Now, as Mathis eased the white convertible into a parking space at the Galt, he asked Namath again.

"I got films to watch," the quarterback explained.

"That's the only excuse I'll take," Mathis said.

On one of the buses returning from the Colt practice, Harry Hulmes, their general manager, turned to Bobby Boyd, the wise, balding cornerback.

"What," asked Hulmes, "can the Jets do to our defenses?"

"We haven't played any club with two better receivers than Sauer and Maynard," said Boyd, who would be covering Maynard much of the time. "We haven't seen anybody as fast as Maynard. He's got great speed."

Out by the Galt pool, Rocky Rochester was sitting with his brother Phil and Babe Parilli.

"I really don't want to go back to high school," Phil was saying. "I don't need a diploma."

"You might think you don't," Parilli said, "but you need that diploma, and a *college* diploma."

"What for?"

"So that when you go to look for a good job, a company will let you apply. If you don't have that diploma, some companies won't even bother to let you fill out an application blank. It's an automatic no."

"Automatic?"

"Ask your brother," Parilli said.

"He's right," Rocky said.

"You mean they won't even talk to me if I'm looking for a job?"

"Not even 'hello'," Parilli said.

Near the beach, Winston Hill stared silently at the surf sliding across the sand. Every so often, the 280-pound offensive tackle would grit his teeth and inhale deeply, his huge chest expanding as if it were about to burst.

"What's wrong?" Matt Snell asked him.

"Nothing, man, nothing," Hill replied.

In his own way, Winston Hill was preparing for his reintroduction to Ordell Braase, the defensive end who had chased him out of the Colts' camp in 1963.

Joe Namath had phoned his mother, Rose Szolnoki, at her Beaver Falls home.

"When are you arriving?" the quarterback asked. "What flight will you be on?"

"Joe," she said, "I'm so worried. All I've read about the last couple weeks are all the planes that have been hijacked to Cuba, and I'm so afraid that will happen to my plane. I know it's silly, but I can't help it. I've got my ticket, and I've got all my clothes packed, and I even got my permanent today, but I'm so worried about the hijacking."

"If that's the way you feel, then you better not come," he said gently. "It's not worth all that worrying."

His gift of the gold brooch with the twelve diamonds would be delayed more than a week after the Super Bowl.

"You can watch the game on television," he said. "We'll win by the same score on TV as we will here."

Lucy Ewbank was getting dressed for dinner when she reached into her jewelry box for a pearl necklace. But in picking it up, she fumbled it, and it clattered across the top of the wooden dresser.

"Weeb," she said, "I'm nervous already. I've never been this nervous."

"Calm down," her husband said gently. "We're going to win this game."

In the lobby, Randy Rasmussen was glowering at Doug Schustek, a television producer.

"I'm warning you," Rasmussen said, "if Billy Ray Smith is there, I'm walking out."

"He won't be there," Schustek said. "Believe me, none of the Colts will be there."

Throughout the season, Schustek had produced a *Jets Huddle* weekly television show. Kyle Rote, an NBC announcer, conducted it, using the outstanding players of the previous game as his guests. But for his Super Bowl show, Schustek had arranged for the appearance of the five offensive linemen whom Joe Namath would depend on for protection—Winston Hill, Bob Talamini, John Schmitt, Rasmussen, and Dave Herman.

Several minutes earlier, Herman had informed Schustek that he was not making the trip to Miami, where the show was to be taped.

Herman had heard, incorrectly, that Bubba Smith was to appear on the show, and despite Schustek's assurance, he refused to go. Rasmussen felt the same way about Billy Ray Smith, his Colt opponent.

"I'll go," Rasmussen was telling Schustek now, "but if he's there, I leave."

Of all the Jet regulars, 23-year-old Randy Rasmussen, the youngest regular, was the most obvious victim of the Super Bowl pressure. Other players had been able to control that pressure, or hide it, but he couldn't. His freckled face had tightened into a grim mask, perhaps because he was about to oppose the idols of his boyhood.

"The Colts played in the first pro game I ever saw on TV," he once said, "and after that, they were my team."

At the time, he was a youngster in Elba, Nebraska, a town of 184 residents, where his family raised cattle and grew corn on a 600-acre farm. He had to be up at six-thirty each morning to feed the cattle before boarding the school bus, and in the afternoon, he had other chores. During the winter, the temperature often dropped below zero.

"Once," he has said, "it was forty-two below zero. I'll always remember that."

His class at Elba High School consisted of fifteen students and there were only five in the class behind him.

"We played eight-man football," he once said, "and I was a big running back."

When he entered Kearney State in his home state, he was molded into a lineman by Al Zikmund, his coach who had been a Nebraska teammate of George Sauer, Sr., more than three decades earlier. Zikmund tipped Sauer to Rasmussen's potential, and the Jets selected him on the twelfth round of the 1967 draft.

"I'd never been out of the state of Nebraska before," he recalls, "and when I got to that Jet training camp in Peekskill, I looked around at all the animals and wondered what I was doing there. But when you get the pads on, it's just football like anywhere else."

Not long after that, Sam DeLuca, the regular left guard, required knee surgery that ended his career. Rasmussen had his opportunity. He made the most of it, although he faltered late in the season, prompting Ewbank to make the Talamini trade. Rasmussen and Talamini alternated throughout the 1968 season, but in the championship game, when Herman was moved to tackle, the 255-pound Rasmussen was inserted at right guard.

"He was great against the Raiders," Ewbank said after that game. "He took Birdwell out of the game."

But now, in the car on the trip to the Miami television studio, Randy Rasmussen had forgotten Dan Birdwell, the Raider tackle. He was thinking only of Billy Ray Smith, a ten-year veteran and ten years older, and wondering if Schustek had conned him, wondering if his Colt opponent really would be on the show.

"He's pretty big, he's taller than me, and he's older," Rasmussen confessed, "and seeing him there might scare me out."

Schustek had been telling the truth. None of the Colts were in the WCKT-TV studio, but he had arranged for audio tapes of Earl Morrall, Johnny Unitas, Bubba Smith, and Ordell Braase. When the show's director, Chuck Bachrach, ordered the Morrall and Unitas tapes played, the Jet linemen were interested, but not involved.

Next rumbled the deep voice of Bubba Smith, who had been asked to comment on Joe Namath's bad knees:

"We're well aware of the fact that he has two bad knees, but I don't think it has any bearing on the way we're going to tackle him. Our main objective is to get to the quarterback, and a lot of times, we ain't going to be able to get to his legs. In other cases, you're going to get there, real low, and you might get a shot at his legs. But me, I don't go down that far. I'm going for his upper body. Personally, I would never try to hurt him because to get a guy like that out of the game would be a loss to the AFL."

Suddenly, the voice of Ordell Braase boomed out of the ceiling loudspeaker.

"He's a big tackle," Braase was saying about Winston Hill. "He sits well, he's quick, and he's mobile."

In his chair, Hill's head snapped up, and he jerked his hands into fists.

"I think he opens up the inside a little bit," Braase continued, "but if I can get to the outside fast enough, I can beat Winston Hill and get to Joe Namath."

The voice stopped. But for several seconds, Winston Hill remained transfixed.

Bake Turner emerged from the Rum House with a gorgeous brunette hanging onto his arm. Across the lobby, John Dockery smiled. "For quality," the Harvard man whispered, "I have never seen dates to match what ol' Bake has shown me down here."

Bill Baird was driving back from the Dania Jai Alai Fronton near the Fort Lauderdale airport.

"Only lost three dollars," he was saying. "Not bad for a night's entertainment. Not too bad."

The Jets' free safetyman and his wife, Louise, had been there with several teammates and their wives, and now, as he drove away, she noticed a Volkswagen ahead of them.

"Remember the last VW we were behind?" she said.

"I sure do," he replied. "I might never forget it."

They had come down from New York for the Super Bowl with the Maynards in the flanker's car. The men had shared the driving. Going through Richmond, Virginia, on Interstate 95, Baird was behind the wheel when the tiny Volkswagen appeared to be easing toward an exit on the right, but suddenly it veered back into the inside lane, skidded on the wet pavement and went off the road. Baird had enough time to weave past the skidding Volkswagen, but with several pairs of headlights in the rearview mirror, he judged it wiser to continue on rather than stop.

"He either dozed off, or he had been drinking," Baird was saying now. "I wonder what happened to him."

Fortunately for the Jets, nothing had happened to their free safetyman or their flanker. At the age of 29, little Bill Baird was about to oppose the Colts in what had been a strange odyssey for him. As a senior at San Francisco State in 1961, he had been ignored by all the teams in the NFL, the AFL, and the Canadian Football League.

"I got form letters from the Oakland Raiders and the Montreal

Alouettes," he once said, "and the Chicago Bears talked to me about a tryout, but nothing happened."

None of the teams drafted him, and none of them approached him about signing as a free agent. But the next fall, when he was a physical-education teacher at a San Francisco high school, he was offered a tryout by the Colts when they appeared at the school's field for a workout the day before their game with the Forty-Niners.

"Go out there," said Weeb Ewbank, then the Colt coach, "and see if you can cover some of our receivers."

He had to cover the best—Raymond Berry and R. C. Owens on one side, Lenny Moore and Jimmy Orr on the other. Throughout the tryout, some of his high-school students cheered him on from the grandstand.

"It was very embarrassing," he would say later. If the students embarrassed him, the Colts did not. That night he signed a contract, although he was not to join the Colts until the 1963 training camp. When he arrived, Ewbank was gone and the Colts had drafted a promising defensive back, Jerry Logan of West Texas State.

Don Shula preferred to keep Logan, but he recommended that Baird contact the Jets.

"The reason we didn't keep him," Shula has said, "was his size— too small, too light."

But Baird's instincts prompted another endorsement from Charlie Winner, then an assistant coach in charge of the Colt defensive backs and now the St. Louis Cardinal head coach. Winner had another reason to be loyal to Weeb Ewbank. He had married one of Ewbank's daughters. At the time, Baird reported to the Jets at 168 pounds. But in the years since then he has filled out to 183, and although he only stands 5 feet 10 inches tall, he immediately moved in as a Jet regular. In one of the freaks of pro football, all four of the Jets' starting defensive backs joined the team as free agents. Now, as Bill Baird turned into the wide concrete driveway of the Galt, he glanced at his watch.

"Plenty of time," he said. "Twenty minutes until the curfew."

"I hope you sleep better tonight," his wife said. "No dreams."

The previous night, he had dreamt that whenever a Colt receiver was running at him in the Super Bowl game, the front rim of his white Jet helmet dropped across his eyes, blinding him. Over and over it happened until he awoke in a sweat.

THURSDAY, JANUARY 9

"We're Going to Win, I'll Guarantee You"

After breakfast, Dave Herman and his wife, Leah, were strolling through the lobby.

"It's so nice out today," she said, noticing the sun glistening on the pool's green water. "Why don't you go up and put on your swimming trunks and lie on the beach."

"I'm not here for a vacation," he replied sharply. "I'm here to work."

Out by the pool, Steve Thompson was lifting his husky little son, Ole, on his right foot. Behind the big rookie defensive end, Dr. Nicholas smiled.

"Still exercising your knee?" the doctor asked.

Thompson turned and grinned. Of all the Jets, he had the most vivid recent memory of the blue uniforms the Colts would be wearing. He had opposed those uniforms in a game between the Jet rookies and the Colt rookies at Baltimore in late July, and he had been a casualty. His right knee had required cartilage surgery.

For several months, he had wondered how it would hold up under contact.

Activated for the game in San Diego, he was assigned to the kickoff unit. Racing downfield under the ball, he suddenly tumbled. He had been whacked across his surgical knee from behind—he had been clipped, one of football's most dangerous infractions because of the possible damage it can do to a player's knee.

Slowly, almost afraid to arise, the 6-foot 5-inch rookie got up and put the weight of his 245 pounds on his right leg.

The knee had survived. Now, as he played with his son, Steve Thompson was waiting for another crack at those people in the blue uniforms.

Johnny Unitas was sitting on a parking attendant's stool outside the Statler Hilton entrance when an elderly man recognized him.

"Aren't you Johnny Unitas?" the man asked.

"Yes, sir, I am," the quarterback replied.

"I used to watch you all the time," the stranger said. "You were a great one. I really enjoyed watching you."

"Thank you," Unitas said, politely.

"Do you think you'll get in the game for a minute or two? You were a great one. I'd sure like to see you get in for a bit. I sure enjoyed watching you play."

"I don't know, sir. That's strictly up to them."

The morning before, Joe Namath had refused to be interviewed by "writers I don't know, because there's been too much crap written about me already." But today, in the glare of the sun, he had sprawled by the pool and chatted pleasantly with several newsmen, most of whom he didn't know.

But now, in the darkness of the noon meeting, he resumed studying films of the Colt defense.

"We can't let them jump around," he was telling George Sauer, Jr., "we've got to control *them*."

"We can do it," Sauer said. "If we execute, we can beat this team, we can beat the hell out of them. Their defense doesn't offer as big a challenge as Oakland's did."

And every time he realized that victory was attainable, he tensed with the enormity of it all.

Over at the Statler Hilton, big Bubba Smith was walking toward the buses that would take the Colts to practice.

"I have a bundle of respect for Joe Namath, he's a damned good quarterback, an exceptional quarterback," he said, "but a football player who's real good doesn't have to talk. The Green Bay Packers were real champions. They never talked. They never had to. This is the way I visualize all champions—solemn, dignified, humble."

He paused before boarding the bus, his 6-foot 7-inch, 295-pound body almost as big as the open door.

"My father coached me at Charlton Pollard High School in Beaumont, Texas, and he taught us to be humble off the field. Inside, I've got to feel I'm the best, but if I tell you that I'm the best, then I'm a fool."

On the beach at the Galt, a local newspaperman suggested to the Jet wives that they arrange a volleyball game with the Colt wives.

"No chance," one of them said.

"Why not?" the newsman asked.

"We'd have to have our husband's expenses paid for by the club."

"And *we*," another said, "would be 18-point favorites over them."

After practice had opened with calisthenics, Jim Turner, his round boyish face set in his intense mask and a square-toed football shoe on his right foot, strode toward the goal posts at the far end of the field. Tall at 6 feet 2 inches but carrying a thick 205 pounds, he is known as "Tank" to his teammates. Throughout the season, Thursday had been his day to work on his field-goal kicking. Alongside him was Babe Parilli, his ball-holder and psychologist.

"It's just another game," Parilli was saying as he knelt at the

32-yard line. "No need to change anything. Let's keep doing things the way we have. I'll tilt the ball the same way, and you kick the same way. And besides, you're better than their guy."

Jim Turner had been better than *anybody* in 1968. He had set a season record for pro football with 34 field goals. In leading the AFL in scoring, he totaled 145 points to establish a record for a kicker. His field goals had provided the victory margin in three games, including a 25–21 triumph over the Buffalo Bills when he booted six, tying the AFL record. In the championship game with the Raiders, his two field goals eventually had made the difference, 27–23.

"All right," Weeb Ewbank was saying now. "Let's go, we've got a lot of work to do out here."

Kneeling on his left leg, Parilli pointed to a spot on the grass where he would place the ball. His arms swinging, his head down, Turner stared at that spot. Seven yards ahead, at the 25, John Schmitt hunched over the ball. Around him, offensive and defensive players were deployed in a mock formation.

"Are you ready?" asked Parilli.

Turner nodded, and Parilli extended his arms toward Schmitt and opened his hands. With a lurch of his shoulders, Schmitt snapped the ball in a smooth spiral into Parilli's hands. Quickly, mechanically, precisely, he spotted the ball, its laces facing the goal posts. Quickly, mechanically, precisely, Turner, peeking to see the ball enter Parilli's hands, took a step with his right foot, another with his left and swung his square-toed right shoe into the ball about 2 inches below the middle. With a thunk, the ball spun end over end, high against the blue sky, above the crossbar and through the 18-foot 6-inch space between the uprights.

"Allrriigghhtt!" his teammates yelled. "Way to kick, Tank."

Their teammates appreciated the kicking trio's artistry. From the moment Schmitt snaps the ball to the moment Turner kicks if out from under Parilli's right forefinger, not more than 1.2 seconds should elapse. If it does, the ball is likely to be blocked. Now, Turner kicked four more between the uprights from the 32. Moving back to the 37, he kicked five in a row, his teammates shouting as each ball soared successfully.

"Let's try the 42," said Parilli.

After three consecutive successful kicks from there, Turner turned and walked away.

"That's enough," he told Ewbank.

At the age of 27, he was a seasoned specialist, but his success had come hard. Out of Utah State, where he had been a rollout quarterback, he was drafted in 1963 by the Washington Redskins of the NFL, but they preferred to keep Bob Khayat as their place-kicker. After being cut, Turner returned to his home in Crockett, California, where he would attend San Francisco State to complete work on his teacher's certificate. When the Jets played an exhibition game in nearby Oakland, he contacted Ewbank for a tryout.

"Come to the game," Ewbank said, "and we'll look at you afterward."

The Jets lost, a preview of their 5–8–1 record that season. But when Youell Field had cleared, Turner—with his brother Jack holding the ball—kicked in a private audition for Clive Rush.

"This guy can do it, Weeb," Rush reported. "He made three out of four from the 52."

At the time, the AFL had a 33-man player limit, and Ewbank could not afford the luxury of a place-kicking specialist. He used Dick Guesman, a defensive tackle.

"But keep your leg in shape," Ewbank told Turner, "and I'll be in touch with you in the spring."

When the Jets assembled for their 1964 training camp, Jim Turner was with them. He used a unique style of punching the ball rather than following-through in the classic manner. But it was effective, and soon he was established as the place-kicker. But he had to be ready as an emergency quarterback, tight end, and flanker. With his sensitive temperament, he resented his versatile role. He considered himself to be a specialist, and he wanted to be treated like one. During the 1968 season, he finally was.

He had earned his stature. His blonde wife, Mary Kay, had helped him earn it. When he had practiced during the off-seasons, she had held the ball for him. Usually, to avoid the noonday sun, they would go in the early morning or at twilight to the empty field at John Swett High School in Crockett, where he had starred. The first time she had held the ball with her slender feminine forefinger, she had flinched as he approached, and the ball had wobbled.

"Don't do that," her husband said. "If I kick, and the ball's not there, I can hurt myself."

When she realized that a professional place-kicker does not kick anybody's finger, she relaxed. The workouts strengthened his right leg. In his leisure hours, he would fish for striped bass and salmon.

"The stripers come in from the Pacific Ocean, 25-pounders," he has said. "They're so strong they'll straighten a stainless steel hook or break it in half."

Or he would dive for abalone, which must be 7 inches across the shell to be taken legally. And then, only five are permitted to be pried with an iron off the rocks in one day.

"I once got three on one trip down," he has said. "I can hold my breath under water for about three minutes."

The stripers and the abalone are his hobby, but place-kicking is his profession. And it's not always fun. When the Jets were trailing the Buffalo Bills in New York by 2 points with less than four minutes remaining, he walked away from his teammates on the sideline and studied the situation that soon would confront him.

"I had to check the angle," he said later, "and how the wind would affect it. The wind is always blowing at Shea Stadium."

In the huddle, his teammates usually talk to him, trying to relax him. But this time they were silent. So was Parilli.

"I really felt the pressure," Turner would say later. "That silence in the huddle really made me aware I had to do it."

He did, booting the ball from the Bills' 35 to lift the Jets into a 22–21 lead. In the final minute, he would add his sixth field goal that rainy afternoon, tying the AFL record in a 25–21 victory. And when it was over, Bobby Sharp, the assistant equipment manager, had reached for his shoes to towel them clean.

"Don't touch them, Bobby," he said. "Nobody touches my shoes. Nobody."

Now, after his practice, he tenderly placed his kicking shoe into his locker, and he entered the trainer's room.

"I feel a little nauseous," he said.

"What's the matter?" somebody asked.

"I think it's the rich food in the hotel," the place-kicker said. "I'm not used to rich food like this day after day."

Jim Turner departed for his shower, pleased at his perfect performance in practice but aware that he must maintain that form.

"Rich food, hell," a teammate said, winking. "Rich nerves."

Inside his white helmet, the sweat was dripping off John Elliott's chin as he turned to Buddy Ryan.

"Coach," the right defensive tackle said, "in the five-one front, do you want me to line up on the guard's outside shoulder or on his ear?"

"You don't have to be that technical about it," the coach said. "Just line up there and hit somebody."

On the next play, John Elliott did just that, as he had throughout the season. At 243, he wasn't as heavy as most defensive tackles. Nor was he as experienced. He was completing his first full season at the position. As a rookie the previous year, he had been used as a linebacker and defensive end, but he had played the final three games at defensive tackle. When the Jets assembled for their 1968 training camp, Weeb Ewbank's blueprint had him at tackle. By the season opener, Ewbank was raving about him.

"We've really got something in this kid," the coach said. "He can be All-Pro."

Ewbank ordinarily doesn't say that about anybody with such limited experience. He had never even said it about Joe Namath at a similar stage of his career. But he was saying it about John Elliott, a shy, silent Texan with a mop of blond hair.

"He's not too heavy, and we have to keep him fed," Ewbank likes to say, "but he's quick."

As a rookie, Elliott's weight had been around 225, but during the off-season, he added about 25 pounds. When the season opened, he was a solid 246. Although some defensive tackles go as high as 275, there have been equally successful tackles of Elliott's weight. Henry Jordan of the Green Bay Packers was one, Tom Keating of the Oakland Raiders another. Their style is not to overpower a guard but to use speed and deception. In a few months at the position, the 24-year-old Elliott had mastered that style.

His agility helped. As a youngster growing up in Warren, Texas, not far from Houston, he high-jumped 6 feet 5 inches.

"I weighed 205 when I did it," he recalled. "That might be a record for somebody that heavy."

But in Texas, where football is more a religion than a sport, his accomplishments as a fullback and linebacker were more important. He moved on to the University of Texas as a teammate of George Sauer, Jr., Pete Lammons, and Jim Hudson, and the Jets selected him as their seventh-round choice in the first combined draft of the two leagues in 1967. Quickly, he had justified Ewbank's prediction. The week before, he had been selected as a member of the Eastern Division squad for the AFL All-Star Game.

"Only two tackles in the AFL really rush the passer," Buddy Ryan often mentioned. "One of them is Buck Buchanan of Kansas City, and the other is John Elliott."

But now, after John Elliott worried about whether to line up on the guard's shoulder or ear, Buddy Ryan walked over to where Weeb Ewbank was surveying practice.

"I think," he said to the head coach, "John's more tense than any of them."

Suddenly, the coach had another concern. Emerson Boozer had dived for a sideline pass and now, as he arose, he was staring painfully at the little finger on his right hand.

"Jeff," he was calling, "Jeff, look at this thing."

Jeff Snedeker, Dr. Nicholas, and Weeb Ewbank hurried to him as he held the pinky in its normal position. But then he let it go, and it drooped unnaturally. He was unable to control the movement in it, and he was understandably worried. So was Weeb Ewbank. But Dr. Nicholas remained calm.

"The tendon went," he said. "We can tape it to the next finger and it'll be all right."

But the doctor's assurance did not soothe the halfback. He glowered in annoyance.

"Damn," he said. "I just got a new pinky ring—white gold with a cluster of diamonds. Christmas present from my wife. Damn, now I won't be able to wear it."

Most of the players had departed, but Joe Namath and Matt Snell were in the trainer's room.

"You first, Matt," said Dr. Nicholas, "because we'll be working on Joe quite a while."

Stoically, the fullback sat on the rubbing table as the doctor prepared to aspirate his right knee. It had required cartilage surgery early in the 1967 season.

"All right," the fullback said as the doctor approached with the needle, "do what you have to do."

About three ounces of the beer-colored fluid appeared in the black-trimmed plastic syringe.

"That's the most you've ever had," the doctor said. "You must be really running hard in the practices."

Now it was the quarterback's turn. On a nearby tray, the needles and syringes had been readied. In about seventy-two hours, Joe Namath would be on the field in the Super Bowl game, his success depending on how he was able to maneuver on his crippled knees. The less pain, the easier it would be for him to maneuver. At present, the doctor was preparing to minimize the pain in those knees.

"Five of them," Namath said, staring at the syringes. "That's a record."

Sitting halfway down the rubbing table, Namath held his legs flat in front of him. His arms behind him, a towel across his middle, the quarterback tightened as the doctor approached his left knee. That was the one with the inflamed tendon. In the syringe was Novocaine, and the doctor inserted the thin 1-inch long needle below the knee-cap. When the Novocaine disappeared, the doctor unscrewed the empty syringe but left the needle protruding.

"What now?" the quarterback said.

"No need to stick you with two needles, I'm just changing the syringe," he said, smiling. "I'm not a sadist."

"Hudson should hear you say that."

The doctor picked up another syringe with a colorless liquid in it.

"Not yet," the quarterback said. "Give the Novocaine time to work."

"Stop moaning," the doctor said, still smiling. "Diabetics do this every day."

In the new syringe was 25 milligrams of Prednisone, which would relieve the pain in the inflamed tendon for several days. When it vanished into the knee, the doctor withdrew the needle.

"Now we'll tap the right one again," the doctor said.

"Not we, you," Namath said. "Don't give me that we."

As on the previous Saturday, about two ounces of fluid were obtained from the right knee through the 3-inch needle.

"Now the left knee again," the doctor said.

This time the needle pierced the skin near the back of the outside of the knee. First the Novocaine. Then the change of syringe.

Then another 25 milligrams of Prednisone to shrink the inflammation in the bursal sac.

"That's it," the doctor said.

"Look at them," Namath said, laughing at the needles and syringes that had been tossed in the wastebasket. "Will you look at all those needles."

"How about another one?"

"For what?" Namath said.

"For your thumb. Will you need one on Sunday for your thumb?"

"No, it might affect my feel for the ball."

The doctor agreed. As the quarterback limped away, the doctor gave him a bottle with red pills to decrease the pain in his left knee. The doctor picked up another bottle with identical red pills and delivered it to Weeb Ewbank.

"What're these for?" the coach asked.

"Your hip," he replied. "Butazolidin."

Jimmy Orr, the little Colt split end, remembered Don Maynard from the Blue-Gray game, a college all-star contest, a decade earlier. "I roomed with him there," Orr was saying, "and he used Mexican dimes for quarters in the pay phones."

In private, Randy Beverly's cool melted quickly. On previous evenings, rather than get dressed for dinner in the Bimini Room, he and his wife, Ruth, had brought take-out orders to their room. Finding that unsatisfactory, they had ordered room-service. But tonight, his wife presumed, they would attend the team barbecue party by the pool.

"No," her husband snapped, "I don't want to go."

"You can't crawl into a shell," she scolded. "You can't sit in here by yourself all the time. It'll do you good to get out and be around other people. You've got to get this game off your mind. You can't stay here all the time."

"If you weren't here, I could."

"This hasn't been any vacation for me," she said.

"I wish you hadn't come."

"I wish I hadn't, either, but I'm here, and *I'm* going to the barbecue. Are you going with me?" The cornerback broke into a slow, soft smile, "Maybe you're right," he said, hoping to forget Jimmy Orr for the next few hours. "All right, let's go."

Near the pool, the players and wives were assembling for the barbecue.

Originally, the idea had been to have a hot-dog roast on the beach, an excuse for all the members of the Jet family to be together. But it had expanded into a more elaborate party and now, in the twilight, the waitresses began to set the long buffet table with platters of spare ribs, fried chicken, pot roast, baked beans, sliced tomatoes, and various salads. Not far away, a bartender was tapping a barrel of beer.

Just about everybody was dressed casually, but when Joe Namath appeared, he had on a shiny soft green suit.

The quarterback was on his way to the Miami Touchdown Club banquet, where he would receive an award as "the Outstanding Professional Football Player of 1968," but he had stopped for a plate of food and a beer. It was as if he wanted to make sure that his teammates realized that, as the offensive captain, the team party was as important to him as his banquet honor elsewhere.

"There was a time," one of the players said, "when Joe wouldn't have bothered to stop by with us."

Soon he had to leave, but the others understood. The barbecue continued with the hum of conversation at the tables among the palm trees. The players had agreed to chip in and split the bill, at about $10 a couple, but now John Free stood near the pool and called for attention.

"I would like everybody to know," the traveling secretary announced, "that Mike Martin wants everybody to be his guest here tonight."

The applause embarrassed the 25-year-old son of Townsend Martin, one of the Jets' owners. As an heir to his family's millions, he could afford to pay the bill, and they knew that. Throughout the season he had impressed the players with his serious manner as the club's assistant business manager, and now he had impressed them with his gesture.

"Biggest dinner tab I ever picked up," he would say, proudly. "Four hundred and thirty dollars."

In the Doral Hotel on the Ocean, the Governor of Florida, Claude Kirk, Jr., was presiding at his party for the visiting dignitaries and newsmen. Not far from the buffet table, with its roast beef and lobster, Norm Van Brocklin, the coach of the Atlanta Falcons and one of the most famous NFL quarterbacks, was talking to a group of sportswriters.

"On Sunday," said Van Brocklin in his assured manner, "Joe Namath will be playing in his first pro game."

Halfway to Miami, on Interstate 95, Joe Namath was sipping Johnnie Walker Red out of a paper cup in the front seat of a turquoise Cadillac sedan. Behind the wheel was Joe Fucile, a 42-year-old used-car lot manager who was driving the quarterback to the Touchdown Club banquet.

"This your car?" Namath asked.

"No, it's my wife's," Fucile replied.

"Something's wrong with the steering?"

"She doesn't drive it this fast."

"Try to keep it on the road," Namath said. "I got someplace I have to be Sunday."

"I want to be there, too," Fucile said.

The quarterback laughed. Their casual conversation continued, and soon, the sedan eased into the driveway of the Miami Springs Villas, where the banquet would be held. Inside, in the red-and-gold decor of the oak-panelled King Arthur's Room, about six hundred people had gathered at long tables. When the quarterback saw them, he was surprised.

"I thought there'd be about two hundred," he whispered.

Back at the Galt, the barbecue was about over. The barrel of beer was empty. Only scraps of food remained on the long buffet table. Several of the players and their wives had drifted inside the hotel, but a few remained among the tables that were stationed between the palms. At one of them was linebacker Ralph Baker's wife, Betsy, with Janet Johnson and Dotty Hampton.

"How's your voice, Dotty?" asked Betsy.

"I'm always in great voice," said the equipment manager's wife. "You know that."

"Greater love hath no friend than to stand next to you at the National Anthem."

"I never heard Dotty sing," said Janet.

"You haven't missed much," said Betsy, her companion at Shea Stadium. "You're not going to sing the National Anthem on Sunday, are you?"

"I certainly am," Dotty said. "Loud and clear."

"Sing it now," Janet said. "Sing it right here."

"Not here," suggested Curley Johnson. "Up on the diving board, sing it up there."

"I'll do that," Dotty Hampton said.

At the other end of the pool, the little blonde mother of five stepped out onto the end of the diving board. In her scratchy voice, she began, "Oh, say can you see . . ." When she finished, Curley Johnson stared up at her.

"Now jump," he said.

"In my clothes?" she said.

"I hope so," he said.

"Don't jump for nothing," Betsy Baker said, remembering Don

Maynard's escapade at Oakland two years before. "Make them put up some money."

About $35 soon was collected by Joanne Schmitt. "That's not enough," said Betsy. "Don't do it for less than $50."

"I'll wait," Dotty said.

Nearby, her husband Bill stared up at his wife, who was wearing new floral-print bell-bottom pants.

"You'll ruin your new pants," Bill said.

"That's all you care about, my new pants," she said laughing. "You don't care if I drown."

Suddenly, from near the lobby, John Free's voice pierced the dark glow around the pool.

"Jeff Snedeker," called the traveling secretary.

Recognizing the voice, and with mischief in his eyes, Larry Grantham spun in his chair.

"John Free," the linebacker said. "C'mere, John Free, I want to tell you something."

John Free, the foil, had heard that tone before. Despite the shadows, he noticed Grantham and Rocky Rochester and Curley Johnson and Pete Lammons and John Elliott approaching him slowly from different directions. He realized that he was about to be tossed into the pool.

In his wallet were some $2,000 worth of personal checks from various Super Bowl ticket-buyers.

"And all I could think of," he would confess later, "was falling into that pool, and the ink running on those checks, and I wouldn't have known who paid for what."

Terrified, he raced through the lobby and hid in the manager's office next to the registration desk.

"Don't tell anybody that I'm here," he whispered to Sally Schwind, the night clerk. "It's a matter of life and death."

After a few minutes, John Free emerged, alive and dry, and more important, with his checks dry.

"I ran those 100 feet faster than any flanker in football," he would say. "I saved $20 a foot."

Outside, the moment had been lost. Dotty Hampton climbed down from the diving board, her pants dry.

On the dais at the Touchdown Club banquet, Joe Namath leaned down every so often and sipped scotch out of a napkin-wrapped old-fashioned glass while the other speakers needled him. Eventually, he was presented with his trophy as the season's outstanding professional football player by Milt Woodard, the AFL president who had scolded him for drinking champagne in a championship clubhouse celebration and had earlier suggested he shave the Fu Manchu.

Then the quarterback, arising on his needle-pierced knees, looked out at the audience.

"This isn't an award for me," he began. "Had it not been for my parents and my family, and my high-school coach, Larry Bruno, and my coach at Alabama, Paul Bryant, and many other people, starting with Mr. Werblin and continuing with Weeb Ewbank and our new owners, who are doing a great job, and all my teammates, I wouldn't be here.

"This should be a most valuable player award for the entire team.

"You can be the greatest athlete in the world but if you don't win those football games, it doesn't mean anything. And we're going to win Sunday, I'll guarantee you.

"When we won the AFL championship, a lot of people thanked the wives.

"I'd like to thank all the single girls in New York, they deserve just as much credit. They're appreciated just as much," he continued, pausing to sip his drink. "You fellows out there under 21, this ginger ale is good stuff. But I'd like to clear something up right now. Some people seem to think that I drink J&B scotch. That's not true, it's Johnnie Walker Red. But anytime you want me to sit down, I will."

In the audience, a voice shouted, "Sit down."

"That must be a guy from Baltimore," the quarterback barked back. "Maybe Lou Michaels. But everybody around the Colts is annoyed because I said that Earl Morrall wasn't as good as Daryle Lamonica of the Oakland Raiders, but those are my feelings, and I think I'm entitled to them, just as reporters are entitled to theirs. And, speaking of reporters, I read where one wrote that our defense can't compare with the Colts.

"Anybody who knows anything about football knows that we have five guys on defense alone better than them.

"And another thing I want to talk about is hair. Mustaches, beards. They're supposed to create a bad image, but who tells the children that it's a bad image, the parents. I shaved off my mustache because I felt like shaving it off; just like I felt like growing it.

"And about the point spread, somebody told me it's 19 now.

"Well, coming down on the plane, it was 17, and Paul Rochester, one of our defensive tackles, said he'd rather be a 17-point underdog than a 19-point favorite, because we were a 19-point favorite twice during the season, and we lost, to Buffalo and Denver, and the Colts should keep that in mind.

"But there's something else to remember about football—the injuries.

"The other day, somebody asked Don Maynard who was the most important member of the team and he said, 'The doctor.' Because the name of the game is Kill the Quarterback, brother."

Quickly, he sat down, taking a fast sip of his drink, and all around him, applause erupted.

In the ceremonies that followed, several autographed footballs were raffled off, and the quarterback tossed them down from the dais to the winners. One of them was won by a young man in a blue shirt and when Namath saw him approach the dais, he momentarily held the ball.

"I don't want to get used to throwing at those blue shirts," he said. When the banquet ended, he signed dozens of autographs.

Outside, the turquoise Cadillac was waiting. This time Namath slid into the back seat because Joe Fucile's red-headed wife, Mildred, was in the front seat with her husband. As he settled himself with another cupful of scotch, he carefully buckled the seat belt.

"All the punishment you take playing football," Mildred said, "and you put on a seat belt."

"Yes, ma'am," the quarterback said. "If you ever drive along the Connecticut Turnpike, you'll see all the wrecked cars on the side, and that's enough to make you wear a seat belt."

"How do you play with your bad knees?" she asked.

"You have to love the game, ma'am. I think all the players love football, really love it, or they wouldn't play it. And about my knees, well, I'm not so bad off. Some people don't have any knees. But the thing is, I love football. I'd love to be a pro coach when I stop playing. I'd really love to be a coach, and I think I'd be a good coach. But I wonder if anybody would take me with my reputation."

She mentioned how dramatic the Jets' victory in the AFL championship game had been, following the interception of a Namath pass in the last quarter by George Atkinson, the Raider cornerback.

"I knocked him out of bounds, remember—kept him from scoring," he said, laughing. "Hell, if I knew they were going to score on the next play, I wouldn't have bothered. But when I tackled him, he said, 'Man, I like to kill you,' and I told him, 'Don't go running off at the mouth at anyone, you're only a rookie'."

Not long after that, Namath and Maynard collaborated for a touchdown in Atkinson's coverage area.

"That's like early in the season, when we played Boston," the quarterback continued. "Don Maynard just missed a pass, and Leroy Mitchell told him, 'You ain't going to beat me this year.' And the next play Maynard caught a long one on him for a touchdown, and he tossed the ball to Mitchell and said, 'I learned a long time ago not to run off at the mouth to anyone.' That skinny Maynard, he's really something else.

"But that championship game, I cried after that game. I've only cried after three games in my life. My sophomore year at Alabama, we beat Florida when they missed a field goal in the last minute, I cried after that. And after the Buffalo game this season, when I threw the five interceptions and they ran three of them back for touchdowns with my father there, I cried then. And then the championship game. Cornell Gordon was falling all over me, and we were crying together, and that was the greatest day, the greatest."

The turquoise Cadillac was on Route A1A now, not far from the Galt.

"Do you people live close by?" the quarterback asked. "Do you live up this way?"

"No," said Mildred Fucile, "we live in South Miami. We've got an hour's drive."

"You didn't have to drive all the way up here," he said. "You didn't have to do that I mean, I appreciate it, but I wish you told me you didn't live near here."

"That's all right," she said. "My horses haven't missed me."

"*Your what?*" the quarterback asked. "Did you say your horses?"

"We've got two riding horses and a mini-mule," she said. "The next time, we'll bring one of the horses and let you ride it back to Lauderdale."

"As long as it's not a colt," the quarterback said.

FRIDAY, JANUARY 10

"I'm Looking to Punish People"

I n the Galt lobby, Ralph Baker slipped 15 cents into the coin slot of the newspaper rack and took a *Miami Herald*. Opening it to the first sports page, he was startled by a big headline: NAMATH GUARANTEES JET VICTORY. Below it was the report of the quarterback's speech at the Touchdown Club banquet.

Baker read it quickly. When he looked up, Bill Hampton was about to join him for breakfast.

"You've got to read this," Baker said to the equipment manager. "You've just got to read this."

Namath's guarantee perhaps had more of an impact on Ralph Baker than on any of the other Jets because the 26-year-old left linebacker would never think of being that boastful. Though a brawny 235 pounds, he's more bashful than brazen. In his second season, he had to be chastised by Weeb Ewbank for gently shoving Jack Kemp, the Buffalo Bills' quarterback, out of bounds.

"You're too nice to everybody," the coach snapped. "You have to be tough, or people will take advantage of you."

In his fifth season, the Penn State alumnus no longer was too nice, but he was too inconspicuous. Baker has been described by Walt Michaels as "steady, dependable, he doesn't make many mistakes." Neither does he make many spectacular plays. For a linebacker to be noticed, he must make an occasional spectacular play.

161

Typical of his fortune was a play that had occurred in the AFL championship game. With the Jets leading, 27–23, and slightly more than two minutes remaining, the Raiders penetrated to the Jet 24-yard line. On a swing pass, Daryle Lamonica tossed the ball backward toward halfback Charlie Smith—thus making it a lateral rather than a forward pass. When the ball rolled off Smith's fingers, it was an incomplete lateral and a free ball, not an incomplete forward pass. Baker, who was responsible for covering Smith on the play, scooped up the ball, and rumbled toward the end zone. But a whistle was blown and he was prevented from scoring.

According to the rulebook, once an incomplete lateral touches the ground, it may be recovered by the opposing team but not advanced.

Baker had provided the Jets with possession on their own 30, and he had destroyed what would be the Raiders' last real threat. But had he scored a touchdown on that lateral, he would have been put on a pedestal with the other Jet heroes of that championship victory. Instead, he was merely *another* Jet who had played well.

"Not being able to run with that ball," he would say later with his shy smile, "is the story of my life."

But his life now revolved about what would happen on Sunday as he finished his breakfast with Bill Hampton and discussed Joe Namath's guarantee.

"I've got a theory," he said.

"What's that?" Hampton asked.

"I think Joe's trying to add to the pressure on himself. He's at his best when the pressure is on. Like in the championship game when we were behind in the last quarter, and like in Houston when we were behind with four minutes to go and he took the offense 80 yards for the winning touchdown. He thrives on pressure, and I think he's creating this pressure on purpose."

"You might be right," Hampton said.

Not all the members of the Jet group looked as optimistically on Joe Namath's guarantee. Among the dissenters was George Sauer, Sr., the director of player personnel, and he approached Gerry Philbin in the lobby.

"This is really going to stir up the Colts," Sauer said.

"When all this talk started, I thought the same thing," the defensive end replied. "But now I'm beginning to think it's good. One of the troubles with the other two AFL teams in the Super Bowl was that they kept saying how great the Packers were, so as not to get the Packers mad. But the trouble was, the AFL players began to believe it themselves."

"Well," said Sauer, "you might have something there."

The newsmen were delighted with a provocative angle. Dozens of them had assembled at the Hilton Plaza, not only for a bloody mary or coffee, but to question Weeb Ewbank and Don Shula. The coaches had been transported to the Super Bowl headquarters for a formal news conference.

"Are you," one of the newsmen asked Ewbank, "as confident as your quarterback?"

"Well," the coach replied, "I don't think any ballplayer should start in a game or even show up if he doesn't think his team has an opportunity to win."

"What about him *guaranteeing* you'll win?"

"That's the way he feels about it, and I'm for him. I wouldn't give a darn for him if he didn't think we could win. I don't think Joe's whistling Dixie at all."

"How," another asked Shula, "do the Colts feel about it?"

"He's given our players more incentive," Shula said, "and I'm sure he's provided extra interest in the game. You very seldom run across a colorful guy like Joe Namath, particularly a guy with that kind of ability. Our football team is conscious of everything that goes on, everything that is written. Joe has made it much more interesting."

"In view of what Joe has said," Shula was asked, "have any of your defensive players suggested kicking off if you win the toss?"

The joking implication was that the Colt defensive players would want to get at Namath as quickly as possible—to humiliate him, to silence him.

"No," said Shula, "but they respect Joe for what they see in the films. It's a challenge to them."

Quietly, almost invisibly, the psychology of the Super Bowl game had been reversed by Namath's brash optimism. Suddenly, the Colt coach had acknowledged that Namath would represent a "challenge" for his team. Originally, the entire challenge had confronted the Jets, or so most people thought.

But not Joe Namath. Coming down on the charter, remember, he had said:

"It's going to be a challenge for us, but it's going to be a challenge for them, too."

Without realizing it, perhaps, Don Shula had agreed with the quarterback.

In his Orange Bowl office, Jim Wilson was checking the concession deliveries.

Wilson supervises the Zum Zum refreshment stands in the stadium, and he had ordered 50,000 hot dogs, 50,000 rolls, 50,000 soft drinks, 15,000 bags of peanuts, 50,000 pounds of ice, 1,000 pounds of french fries, and 500 roast-beef sandwiches. On Sunday, he would have 325 vendors to distribute the food.

"I like the point-spread," he said. "I like a one-sided game. In a close game, people are less likely to leave their seats to get something to eat."

In their noon meeting at the Galt, a "kicking reel" of the Colts on kickoffs, punts, and placements was being viewed by members of the Jets' special teams.

"There, see that," Mark Smolinski was telling his teammates, "see how they cross their men on the kickoff to get the angle on you. We've handled that crossover before. Kansas City and San Diego do it, and Buffalo has used it a few times. You just have to keep your eyes open around you."

Smolinski keeps his eyes open when many players prefer to close them—on the special teams.

He had been a running back with the Colts during Weeb Ewbank's last two seasons there. But when Don Shula took over in 1963, he was cut to make room for Jerry Hill, his teammate at the University of Wyoming who had been hampered for two seasons by injuries. Joining the Jets as a 215-pound running back, he also was employed occasionally as a tight end. But his primary duty now occurred on the special teams, and he had become the captain of them. Out of that duty had emerged his philosophy regarding the most reckless part of pro football.

"On the special teams," he once said, "you've got to hit or be hit. You play with abandon. You turn your body completely loose. It's tough, and you can get hurt, but it boils down to a matter of pride in doing the job. If you do it well, if you hit hard, the hitting becomes contagious and carries over to the offense and defense."

Now, as he watched the Colt special teams, he was hoping the hitting would be contagious on Sunday.

During the morning, Helen Springborn, chic, blonde vice-president of the Jets, had gone with the other wives on a tour of Fort Lauderdale. Now, after lunch with a few of them, she had rejoined her husband Reynolds.

"How are the wives holding up?" he asked.

"They're trying to act happy and smiling," she said, "but I think they all want to throw up."

In the locker room at Fort Lauderdale Stadium, Joe Namath was lacing his white football shoes when John Free approached.

"All those reservations you asked me about yesterday," the traveling secretary said. "They're all set for you."

The hotel reservations had been for Namath's father and brother Bob. John Free isn't responsible for relatives or friends, but he had gone out of his way, as he usually does. Namath's apparent lack of appreciation did not bother him. Accustomed to being the foil for most of the players, he continued toward Weeb Ewbank's office. Several minutes later, he passed the quarterback's locker again.

"Hey, look, John," said Namath, making a big show of holding a chunk of chewing tobacco. "Look at this."

"Don't do it, Joe. I won't let you off the hook on our bet. Even at this late date. Don't do it, Joe."

At training camp in July, Free had been chatting with Namath when the quarterback pinched a small supply of snuff out of a small round container, a habit he had cultivated after he stopped smoking early in 1967.

"That's the filthiest habit a man can have," the traveling secretary snapped.

"It's not too clean," Namath said, "but it keeps me from smoking cigarets."

"It's filthy," Free said. "Anyone with your stature and your looks shouldn't be going around expectorating into a paper cup all the time. It's a filthy habit, and you shouldn't do it. I'll bet you $200 you can't stay off that stuff until the final post-season game."

"You got a bet," Namath said.

Several days later, Free noticed that Namath was chewing tobacco during practice.

"I'll bet you another $100 on chewing tobacco," he said.

"You got it," Namath said, tossing away the tobacco and offering his right hand to seal the bet—$300 total.

"Shake hands with your left hand," Free said in disgust. "You threw that wad of tobacco away with your right."

Now, in the locker room, Namath was holding the chunk of tobacco above his mouth and with a cold, hard look at Free, placed it on his tongue and began to chew it.

"You just lost $100," said Free, "so I owe you a net $100 if you don't go for that snuff until after the All-Star Game a week from Sunday."

Namath smiled, chewing his tobacco. He pulled on his red practice jersey and strode toward the tunnel leading to the field.

"I owe you a net $100, that's all," Free repeated.

Not long after that, John Free strolled through the tunnel to watch practice. As he emerged in the dugout, he noticed a splatter of chewing tobacco on the steps. Out on the field, Joe Namath was *not* chewing tobacco.

"I'm convinced," John Free would say later, "that was his way of thanking me for the reservations I'd made for him."

As it turned out, the traveling secretary lost the other part of the bet. But when he attempted to pay the quarterback the $100, Namath refused to accept it.

Johnny Sample already was thinking of how he would celebrate a Super Bowl victory. "I'll have my first drink," the cornerback told Matt Snell. "I'll have some champagne."

When practice began, Weeb Ewbank was anxious to discover the condition of Don Maynard's sore left thigh. Maynard had assured the coach that his Friday workout would be enough. Now, the slim flanker loped out of the huddle, lined up and listened for the snap signal.

Streaking downfield in his long strides, he suddenly glided to a stop. Dejectedly, he shook his head.

"I felt it again," Maynard told the coach. "I don't want to aggravate it anymore. I'm going inside."

Nearby, his arms folded, Bake Turner, who had been practicing all week at flanker in Maynard's absence, watched him stroll toward the dugout.

"Right then," Turner would say later, "I thought sure that I'd be playing the whole game."

So did most of his teammates, startled by Maynard's sudden departure. And as Ewbank watched the flanker leave, he noticed a stranger near the dugout. Throughout the week, the coach had masked his concern about Maynard, assuring newsmen that the flanker would start. But now Maynard was a questionable, if not doubtful starter. Ewbank would continue to pretend that Maynard was a certain starter, but a *stranger* had seen him pull up and leave the field. The coach hadn't expected the Colts to spy on his practice, but if they dared, the spy would be a complete stranger, somebody Weeb wouldn't recognize. Or suppose the stranger was a newsman who, perhaps innocently, had penetrated the closed practice session.

"Who's that?" the coach asked John Free.

"I don't know," the traveling secretary said. "I never saw him before."

"Find out," the coach ordered.

Moments later, Free returned with his report. The stranger was a photographer assigned to take a picture of place-kicker Jim Turner for an endorsement. Without realizing it, the photographer had infiltrated the closed practice session.

"Tell him," Weeb Ewbank said, "to wait outside."

Soon the workout was over, but Joe Spencer was sending the linemen through their last grass drill. When it ended, most of the players gasped their appreciation. Their torture would not be resumed until training camp. But two players, Winston Hill and Bob Talamini, were dissatisfied.

"Give us a few more," Talamini said.

"We need more work," Hill demanded.

Spencer was astounded. In his sixteen years of coaching, no players had ever requested extra grass drills.

"Save it for Sunday," the coach said.

In the locker room, John Namath chatted with his son. He has been among the players often in four seasons, and many of the veterans knew him and greeted him.

"Hello there, champ," he said to one of them. "I'm going to call you all champs."

"Not yet," another player cautioned. "We haven't beaten them yet. We've got to win."

"You're going to win," the quarterback's father said. "The Raiders were tougher than this team will be. You're the champions of the American Football League, and you'll be the champions of all football."

"I'm sure glad *you* feel that way, too, because Joe's been telling us that all week."

Don Shinnick, the Colts' right linebacker, was at practice when his brunette wife, Marsha, arrived at the Statler Hilton. Awaiting her in their room was a huge bouquet of red and yellow roses. When he returned, he glanced at the roses.

"Did you count them?" he asked her.

"No, should I?" she said, wondering why.

"I mean how many red, how many yellow?" When she did, she discovered that there were thirty-one red roses and ten yellow roses. "That'll be the score," he told her.

Leo Palmieri, the Jets' ticket manager, had arrived from New York but Phil Iselin had suggested that he avoid being around the Galt.

"As soon as everybody sees you," Iselin has said, "they'll all want tickets. And you don't have any more."

Quietly, the 25-year-old Palmieri loafed at the Bal Harbour Inn, several miles away, unknown and unbothered.

Vince Lombardi, who coached the Green Bay Packers to victories in the two previous Super Bowl games, was talking with Morris Siegel of the *Washington Star*.

"Will the Colts win easy?" the sports columnist asked.

"You know where my heart is," answered Lombardi, understandably an NFL loyalist. "But don't be surprised if this doesn't turn out to be a runaway. They are capable of giving them a great fight."

"You mean Namath?"

"He's very dangerous, and he has receivers who can catch the ball."

"How dangerous?"

"I better be going," Lombardi said, smiling. And he departed.

But many months earlier, in assessing the Jet quarterback, Lombardi had said: "His arm, his release of the ball are just perfect. Namath is as good a passer as I've ever seen. From what I've seen on the films, he's a perfect passer."

His wife, Leah, was watching television, but Dave Herman, lying on his bed, was staring at the ceiling.

"I've always been on teams that came in second," he said quietly, "and that's like coming in last."

When he was at Michigan State, the Spartans never qualified as the Big Ten representative for the Rose Bowl, and during his career with the Jets, their best previous finish had occurred in 1967, when they placed second to the Houston Oilers in the AFL Eastern Division.

"This time," he continued, his eyes still fixed on the ceiling, "I'm going to be on a team that wins."

Joe Namath was on the sidewalk outside Howard Johnson's, across the street from the Galt. The quarterback was chatting with Buck Buchanan of the Kansas City Chiefs, who had come in for the game on his way to Jacksonville for the AFL All-Star Game, when Buddy Ryan emerged from the restaurant. With the defensive line coach were his ex-wife, Doris, and their sons, 11-year-old Jimmy and the 6-year-old twins, Rex and Robby.

"Hey, there, Jimmy," the quarterback called. "I want you to meet somebody."

Jimmy had been around the locker room with his father at training camp, and the players knew him. After the introduction to Buchanan, he was hurrying to catch up to his father when he was stopped by two girls who appeared to be in their early twenties. After a brief conversation, he hurried on.

"What did those girls want?" his father asked.

"Oh," the boy said, "they noticed that I knew Joe and they wanted me to introduce them to him. Now why would they want me to do that?"

The weekend had begun. In the Miami International Airport, people poured through the corridors of the terminal, many of them from New York and many of them traveling on package tours—so much for airfare, hotels, *and* a ticket to the Super Bowl game. The wave of airline hijackings to Cuba had concerned some people, but it hadn't stopped many.

"I came down a day early just in case," a man was saying near the Eastern Airlines' luggage area. "If we got hijacked, I'd have time to get in and out of Havana before the game Sunday. And I even brought my passport to save time."

With the people pouring through the terminal, the money was pouring into the Miami area. About $50 million would be spent there over a 10-day period, according to the Miami-Metro News

Bureau estimate. And some scalpers were getting as much as $250 for a pair of tickets.

Five secretaries from the Jets' office in New York had arrived—Janie Seidman, Maria Barone, Kay McDaniel, Bess Eisenberg, and Jeanne Fitzgerald. Now, as they signed the registration cards at the Galt desk, John Free noticed Karl Henke, a reserve defensive lineman who would not be in uniform for the game, sitting alone in the Rum House.

"Karl," the traveling secretary said, "will you do me a favor? It's important for the morale of the office. Will you act as host for our office girls and sit with them for a couple of drinks? Here's $20 for the tab."

Henke agreed. Free ushered the girls to a table, then excused himself. But he was pleased with his hospitality. He had arranged for the secretaries to sit with a big, blond youngster whose handsome looks had captivated airline stewardesses on charter flights throughout the season, and he had left $20 for the tab.

Matt Snell and Emerson Boozer were in their room, watching television, when Snell suddenly flared.

"It makes me mad just to think about it," he said.

"Makes you mad to think about what?" Boozer asked.

"About that matchup in the paper with their backs. How can writers say that Matte and Hill are better than you and me? How can they say that? Booz, if I can't run the ball as well as Hill, and if you can't run it as well as Matte, we're in sad shape."

"We've got to *do* it," Boozer said, quietly.

They had performed brilliantly whenever their knees had let them—Snell with power, Boozer with flash. But they had done it in the AFL and to many people that made a difference. Snell and Boozer had heard the remarks often. It simmered inside both of them, but it has simmered inside Snell much longer.

The fullback had been the Jets' top draft choice in 1964—the first rookie to be selected during Weeb Ewbank's regime, the first rookie to be romanced in Sonny Werblin's spending spree.

Snell also was a third-round choice of the rival New York Giants in the NFL draft, but apparently that was mostly for the nuisance value of forcing Werblin to bid higher. Several months later, a Giant official would be quoted as saying that, even if Snell had accepted their offer, "at that price, there's no guarantee he would have made our club." The implication was that if Snell had not been a star, he would've been cut or traded. But when Snell joined the Jets, his position was undetermined. He had performed at fullback, linebacker, and defensive end during his college career at Ohio State. After viewing Ohio State films, Ewbank decided that he would try Snell first at fullback.

At a solid 220 pounds, Snell responded by running for 948 yards and contributing 393 more as a pass-receiver. He was named the AFL "Rookie of the Year."

In each of his first three seasons, Snell finished among the AFL's top ten in both rushing and pass-receiving, a rare combination for a power runner. But in the opening game of the 1967 schedule, he was cutting upfield at Buffalo when the cleats of his right shoe caught in the turf. His right knee twisted. Without having been hit, he fell. He required surgery to repair cartilage damage.

"I got back for the last few games of the season," he later said, "but I was just there. I wasn't me. I was just somebody in my uniform."

During the 1968 season, the 27-year-old Snell was himself again. He ran for 747 yards, sixth in the AFL, and he earned Ewbank's acclaim as "one of the best pass-blockers I've ever seen." He proved how complete a player he was in a relatively meaningless game with the Cincinnati Bengals, after the Jets had clinched the Eastern Division title.

The Jets were leading, 20–7, in the final quarter as Curley Johnson prepared to punt from the Jets' 30-yard line. Several yards in front of Johnson was Snell, the punter's bodyguard. But one of the Bengals swooped through to block the punt. Another snatched the loose ball and raced toward the goal line. In such a situation, some players might have succumbed to the temptation of not pursuing the Bengal ball-carrier. After all, the Jets were the divisional champions; a Bengal touchdown would not erase the Jets' lead.

Instead, Snell chased the Bengal ball-carrier as though the season depended on it. He caught him from behind at the 2-yard line. Inspired by Snell's play, the defensive unit prevented the Bengals from scoring in a dramatic goal-line stand.

Snell's dedication to football perhaps had been inspired by what a fan had told him one night a few years earlier at a banquet.

"I know why you signed with the Jets," a man told Snell, "because you knew that you couldn't have made the Giants."

Emerson Boozer had experienced a somewhat similar insult. One night, after his 1966 rookie season, he was in Philadelphia visiting Lane Howell, one of the Eagles' offensive tackles. Two other Eagles were there—Bob Brown, the All-NFL offensive tackle, and Nate Ramsey, a defensive back. Also there was Bob Taylor, who had been with the Giants briefly. As a result, Boozer found himself ignored in the conversation that revolved about NFL topics. Particularly annoying to Boozer was Brown's boast of being the best offensive tackle in pro football.

"I handle all the great defensive ends," Brown bragged. "Deacon Jones, Willie Davis, I handle 'em."

"You're going to have trouble with Gerry Philbin," interrupted Boozer, thinking of the Jet-Eagle exhibition game scheduled for that coming summer, "he's the best in our league."

"I'm the best in my league, your league, anybody's league," Brown snapped. "I'll tear Philbin to shreds."

For emphasis, Brown threatened to tear Boozer to shreds right there, but the halfback wisely negotiated an armistice. Boozer is 5-feet 11-inches tall and 202 pounds, with muscles that bulge. But Brown is 6-feet 4-inches tall and 295 pounds, with muscles he hasn't used yet. Several months later, Brown would tell Boozer that Gerry

Philbin is a "fine player," but Brown could afford to be gracious. The Eagles had won the game.

Not long after that, Emerson Boozer suddenly developed into the AFL's most spectacular ball-carrier.

Out of Maryland State, he had been a sixth-round draft choice of the Jets in 1966, and the Pittsburgh Stealers had named him in the NFL selections. He had hoped to be picked by the Giants, and he settled on the Jets because of their New York base. As a rookie, he showed potential. In his second season, he produced 13 touchdowns in the first seven games with a twisting, billiard-ball style of running.

But the next Sunday, he was scissored by two Kansas City Chief tacklers. Suddenly, he couldn't walk.

Surgery was necessary to repair ligament and cartilage damage in his right knee. Dr. Nicholas called it the worst he had ever seen. When he reported to the 1968 training camp, he was issued practice jerseys but his were distinguished by a red cross. The other players knew what the message meant: hands off, don't touch.

His mind also had a red cross on it.

"Just watching football now," he said during training camp, "I see things I never saw before—like pain. I saw Billy Joe get hit in the last game and someone landed across the back of his legs and I saw pain. It startled me. I never looked at football before with that thought in mind. I always heard fans oohing and aahing when someone was really hit, but I couldn't understand it. It had no meaning for me. Solid shots were solid shots, and they were never painful. But now I look at games the way the fans do."

Gradually, he learned that his scarred right knee would withstand the solid shots. He ran for 441 yards and five touchdowns, not spectacular, but an important contribution to the Jet championship.

Now, as the 25-year-old Emerson Boozer looked up from the television set in the room he shared with Matt Snell, he wasn't worried so much about his knee. The knee had survived the season and the championship game. He was more concerned with how the taped fingers on his right hand would hold a ball and with how he would block. Throughout the week, he had slammed into the blocking sled, aiming at the level of the throat of an imaginary Colt, and he had promised Matt Snell that he would "slice 'em in half," meaning his Colt opponents.

Pacing the room, Snell continued to be annoyed with the newspaper matchups with the Colt backs.

"Booz," he said, his eyes flashing, "for the first time in my life, I'm going to be looking for people to run into. I'm going to be looking to punish people."

"Be looking for the goal line, too," Emerson Boozer said.

There was a knock on the door of room 136, and when Weeb Ewbank opened it, Johnny Unitas and his wife, Dotty, smiled.

They had stopped by for a surprise visit with the Jet coach and his wife, Lucy. When he was coaching the Colts, Ewbank had developed Unitas into a master quarterback and, despite his departure, their friendship had endured. They talked about the five Unitas children and about several mutual friends in Baltimore, but they mostly ignored Sunday's game.

"I didn't even ask him how his arm was," Weeb would say later. "That wouldn't have been fair."

After their visit, he escorted them down the hall toward the lobby. He didn't want to be seen publicly with an opposing quarterback, so he shook hands with them near the beauty shop, and the quarterback and his wife strolled on.

Suddenly, through the glass front door, Joe Namath appeared. The young quarterback had met the old quarterback a few years earlier at a banquet in Columbus, Ohio. Quick to recognize each other, Namath and Unitas shook hands. The contrast was evident—the mod, shaggy-haired young pro in the black turtleneck shirt under his black blazer, and the conservative, crew-cut old pro in a gray suit and patterned tie.

During the season, Namath had been asked if he thought he someday would succeed Unitas as the king of the quarterbacks.

"No," he had replied, and when asked why not, he said, with a grin, "because I feel I'm there now."

As a high school player, one of Namath's nicknames had been "Joey U," a takeoff of the "Johnny U" nickname for the Colt veteran. But now, in the lobby, they chatted briefly. While their conversation was pleasant and respectful, it was innocuous. Near the beauty shop, Ewbank stared thoughtfully at them, as if he were a sculptor reflecting on masterpieces he had created a decade apart—one new and shiny and controversial, the other old and worn and almost forgotten.

Soon the quarterbacks parted. Weeb Ewbank turned and hobbled on his cane toward his poolside room.

The invasion of thin portable typewriters, cameras, and tape-recorders was about over. Don Weiss, the slim public-relations director from Commissioner Pete Rozelle's office, had supervised the issuance of credentials to 367 sportswriters, 253 photographers, and 214 radio and TV people—a total of 834. (About 200 newsmen are accredited in Vietnam.) In a pool of 55 newsmen, 49 selected the Colts to win. Cameron Snyder of the *Baltimore Sun* picked the Colts by 47–0, and Tex Maule of *Sports Illustrated* liked the Colts, 43–0.

Now, in the Hilton Plaza's midnight quiet, Weiss chatted with Jim Heffernan, the red-haired NFL information director.

"In their minds," confided Heffernan, who had been with the Colts all week long, "there's no way they think they can lose."

Wearing plaid bermudas, Joe Namath peered through the flickering light of the darkened Governor's Suite. Earlier, his girlfriend, Suzy Storm, a tall long-haired blonde, had arrived from Pensacola Junior College, where she's a student. They had gone to dinner, along with his father, at Sonny Werblin's home, but now the quarterback was munching popcorn with Jim and Wendy Hudson as the one-eyed monster showed the Colt defensive unit operating against the Los Angeles Rams in their final regular-season game.

"See that," he said to Hudson. "Nine men up."

On the wall, the two Colt safetymen, Rick Volk and Jerry Logan, had moved up to the line of scrimmage, joining the four defensive linemen and the three linebackers.

"Now watch," he said.

Although the area down the middle had been vacated, none of the Ram receivers moved toward the clearing. Instead, the Rams used a running play, which the Colts stopped with a swarm of tacklers.

"They ran that play right at the Colts' strength," Namath said. "We won't do that. We'll break those outside receivers to the inside on slants."

On another play the Ram quarterback, Roman Gabriel, was looking for a receiver and finally, in desperation, he threw a pass far downfield. Namath stopped the film and pointed to the top of the movie frame, where a receiver was running straight-ahead.

"See that receiver," he said. "He didn't even turn around to help the quarterback. *Our* receivers turn around."

Play after play, Namath dissected the moves of the Colt defenders, particularly safetymen and linebackers. He tried to recognize the defensive formation they would use from various tipoffs.

"See that," he said once as Volk jumped back from the line of scrimmage. "When I see that, I know it's a zone."

When he put on a reel of the Colts' championship victory, he was surprised when the Cleveland Browns used a running play in which none of their blockers was assigned to Don Shinnick. The linebacker made the tackle.

"That's not sound football," Joe Namath said. "We're going to play sound football."

SATURDAY, JANUARY 11
"I Don't Want to Be a Widow"

Jim Turner had been awake since dawn. The place-kicker had dreamt that on a field-goal attempt in the Super Bowl game, he had booted the ball squarely but it had floated straight up into the air and had dropped almost at his feet. The dream startled him from his sleep, and he had tossed in bed for several hours. Beside him, his wife, Mary Kay, slept peacefully as their room brightened slowly on the cloudy morning.

In another twenty-four hours, it would be the day of the game and for Jim Turner, as for all the Jets, the waiting was almost over.

"We can beat the Colts," the place-kicker would tell an old friend that afternoon. "They're not as good as the Raiders."

But the pressure of the possibility of such a victory placed a burden on Jim Turner, perhaps more than on any other single Jet player. Almost every close game in pro football turns on the success or failure of the field-goal kickers, and while the Jets were optimistic about winning, they believed it would be a close margin. Jim Turner presumably would have to provide that margin.

"Wake up, baby," Jim Turner said to his wife now. "Time to get up."

Jim Turner had to get out of that room and do something. Anything.

At breakfast, Leah Herman stared through the windows of the

Bimini Room at the gray sky. "Look at her," said Dotty Hampton at another table. "I don't know who's more psyched up for Bubba—her or Dave."

Bob Namath, the quarterback's 34-year-old brother, had arrived late last night. Growing up in Beaver Fails, he liked to take his kid brother to the movies. "Every Saturday afternoon and Wednesday night," he says, "starting when Joe was about 9." Now he owns Namath's Lounge in Monaca, Pennsylvania, about six miles east of Beaver Falls. He was sitting with his father out near the Galt pool when he greeted his kid brother.

"I didn't come down here for nothin'," Bob said sharply. "Show me a winner."

"We will," his kid brother said.

John Free was moving through the lobby when he noticed one of the secretaries he had arranged for Karl Henke to host.

"Did you have a nice time last night?" he asked.

"Oh, yes," she replied. "We had a few drinks, and Karl was very nice to us."

"I'm glad he was a good host. I left him money to treat you to your drinks."

"We each paid for our own."

"I left him $20 to do that."

"Oh, he *offered* to pay, but we wouldn't let him. We split the bill."

The noon meeting was brief. The game plan had "crystallized," as Weeb Ewbank liked to say, but for players to know a game plan and to execute it properly were two different things. Particularly for a defensive back, whose mistakes can be so obvious. As they rode in separate buses to the final practice session, Randy Beverly and Bill Baird had the same thought: *Don't be the goat.*

In the Fort Lauderdale Stadium locker room, Bill Hampton was collecting the blue game-plan folders from the players.

The equipment manager would lock them in one of the green trunks. Eventually, in the winter emptiness of Shea Stadium, each would be ripped in half and burned in the ballpark's incinerator—all but two copies, one for offense and one for defense. Weeb Ewbank would keep those for his personal file.

Soon the final practice began with cheers when Jim Turner kicked ten consecutive field goals, five from the 32-yard line, five from the 37. None dropped at his feet.

In the offensive drill, Don Maynard was about to test his sore thigh again. Xylecaine had been injected into the area of the pulled muscle and the flanker had jogged easily to loosen it. Now, his cleats digging tiny chunks of grass out of the turf, he was running his different patterns—a square-out, a square-in, a slant.

"How is it?" Ewbank asked.

"So far, so good," Maynard replied.

"Don't overdo it now."

Not long after that, Maynard was moving downfield when he suddenly slowed to a stop. "What happened?" Ewbank said. "I felt something. I better not run anymore on it."

"Whirlpool it," Ewbank said.

But as Maynard disappeared through the dugout, and as Bake Turner became convinced he would start tomorrow, Dr. Nicholas was reassuring Ewbank of Maynard's availability.

"He just tore a little scar tissue," the doctor said. "He can start tomorrow if you want to use him."

Not long after that, the practice ended. All the preparation had been completed. Sweating freely, Gerry Philbin strolled toward the dugout where a bystander glanced at him.

"Twenty-four hours from now," the man said.

"All the years," the defensive end replied, "and now it's down to twenty-four hours."

At the Colt practice, Ordell Braase stood around in a sweater and slacks. He had been bothered by a muscle spasm in his back, and he didn't want to risk aggravating it. But the 245-pound defensive end assured Don Shula that he would be able to start tomorrow.

"I just need some heat on it," Braase said.

Back at Fort Lauderdale Stadium, two patients awaited treatment by Dr. Nicholas in the trainer's room. Matt Snell would have his puffed knee aspirated again. Two ounces of yellow fluid would appear in the syringe. The medical preparations, like the strategical preparations, had ended, and Dr. Nicholas joined Weeb Ewbank in the coach's office.

"Snell should be in top form," the doctor said. Ewbank nodded, but at the moment he appeared to be more interested in the sports section of the *Miami News*.

"Did you see the Biletnikoff story?" Frank Ramos asked the doctor. "He thinks the wrong AFL team is playing."

Fred Biletnikoff, the flanker of the Oakland Raiders, had terrorized the Jets in the championship game.

"We deserve to be in the Super Bowl," he had been quoted. "We're a much sounder ballclub than New York, and I think that's what bothers us most—we know we're a better team."

Ewbank slowly read the words aloud, then handed the newspaper to the doctor.

"That's the nicest thing," the coach said, "Biletnikoff ever did for us."

Down at the Orange Bowl, preparations had momentarily halted. Throughout the big horseshoe stadium, the national anthem resounded in an unusual rendition—the soft blare of a trumpet pressed to the lips of Lloyd Geisler, the first trumpeter of the National Symphony orchestra in Washington, DC.

Of all tomorrow's pre-game and half-time performers, he would be the only one permitted to rehearse in the stadium today.

With the field soft, a marching band would soften it even more. The field was for football players, not for marching musicians.

When the trumpeter's last note floated away, Mark Duncan, the Commissioner's supervisor of officials, resumed inspecting the field with George Toma, who had been imported from Kansas City to direct the condition of the field and its colorful decorations.

"George," said Duncan, "you're an artist."

"No," he said, "I'm just a groundskeeper."

In her living room, Joe Namath's mother watched Buzzy, the television repairman in Beaver Falls, tinker with her color set.

"It's got to work tomorrow, Buzzy," she said. "It's been on the blink for a week, but it's got to work tomorrow. It's got to work perfectly."

"It will," Buzzy said.

"It better," she said.

Superstition had prevented Phil Iselin or Weeb Ewbank from arranging for the possibility of a post-game victory party. Now John Free cornered Dave Searles, the Galt's convention manager.

"If we win tomorrow," Free explained, "we'd like to hold a party here tomorrow night."

Free outlined a buffet of fried chicken, roast beef, ham, various salads, milk, soft drinks, and beer, plus an open bar.

"And champagne?" Searles asked.

"Lots of champagne," Free said.

"But when will I know for sure?"

"If we win, it's on. That's all I can tell you."

"And if you lose?"

"Then there's no party," Free said. "Then there's no nothing."

In glaring green and white, a larger-than-life-size torso of Joe Namath revolved above the red-and-white marquee proclaiming "Broadway Joe's"—the first of the fast-food restaurants named for the quarterback and situated in Miami not far from the 79th Street Causeway.

Inside, the waitresses and countermen were wearing white football jerseys with a green "12" on each one.

And now, in the late afternoon, a middle-aged couple and their two children strolled into the restaurant. Glancing at the menu that includes a Football Hero, a Quarterback Burger, and a Clubhouse Special, one of the youngsters, a boy about 10, looked at the manager, Buster Hill.

"We're from Baltimore," the boy said.

"Well," said Hill, "it's nice of you to stop by."

"I've got a question."

"Go ahead," Hill said.

"When the Colts win, are you going to take the '12' off and just wear plain white jerseys?"

Mrs. Mary Michaels, spry at 72, had arrived from Swoyersville, Pennsylvania, and she was living at the Galt in a room arranged by her son Walt, the Jets' defensive coach. Two days earlier, at the local Lum's restaurant, equipment manager Bill Hampton had mentioned to Lou Michaels that his mother would be staying at the Jets' hotel, rather than at a neutral site.

"I don't believe it," the Colt place-kicker said, deflated by the information. "She told me she wasn't even coming."

With a flourish, Babe Parilli spread his cards on the table.

"Gin," he announced.

"That's all," Bill Mathis said. "That's all for the season."

"How much am I ahead?" Parilli asked.

From the time they had begun their gin-rummy game at training camp, they had kept a running score through dozens of games during training camp, on planes, in hotel rooms, in locker rooms, and, for the past ten days, at the Galt, where Mathis now was checking the financial statement.

"Twelve-twenty," Mathis said.

"You can afford it," Parilli said, "but don't pay me now. You can buy me dinner when I come to New York some day."

Dr. Nicholas and his wife, Kiki, were having a drink in the Rum House with Andre Kostelanetz, the conductor of the New York Philharmonic orchestra. Small, sharp-featured, with thin gray hair, he had arrived as the doctor's guest for the game. He had attended practice, which he called "the rehearsal," and now he was sipping a vodka and tonic when Joe Namath passed by. The doctor introduced the quarterback to the maestro.

"Tomorrow," the maestro said, "is the grand finale for you."

"And what a surprise ending it's going to be," Namath said.

Earlier in the week, when the appearance of the Apollo 8 astronauts and their families at the game was announced, several strangers had phoned Jim Kensil, the Commissioner's executive assistant. Each offered to stop by and pick up the tickets that had been set aside for the moon-orbiting spacemen.

But the tickets, naturally, had not been entrusted to anyone and now Pete Rozelle had arrived at the Kenilworth Hotel to deliver them personally to Frank Borman, Jim Lovell, and Bill Anders.

"Boy, dad," piped 15-year-old Eddie Borman, seeing the red-and-yellow tickets in the Commissioner's hand, "that trip around the moon was well worth it. We got to go to the Super Bowl game."

The three astronauts, who live in Houston, follow the Oilers, and Borman's two sons, Eddie and 16-year-old Fred, are ballboys for them in the Astrodome. The astronauts and their families would be the guests tonight and tomorrow morning of K. S. "Bud" Adams, Jr., the Oilers' owner, at lavish parties in their honor, but they would truly enjoy the game the most.

"Football," says Frank Borman, "is one of the few things left where you have to keep going when you'd rather stop. It's important to our civilization."

But now, with everyone in the room at the Kenilworth chuckling over Eddie's remark about the moon voyage being "well worth it," the astronauts repeatedly told the Commissioner how much they appreciated his invitation. Whenever he would think of them later, Pete Rozelle would remember how grateful they were.

"They're thanking me over and over," he would say, "when I was grateful to *them* for coming."

In the Howard Johnson's restaurant across the street from the Galt, the Samples were having dinner.

"Dad," his oldest son, John III, said, "you're not going to get beat that bad, are you, Dad?"

"You don't have to worry about that," his father replied. "You don't have to worry about that at all."

He let the children do most of the talking after that, but, as they left, his wife, Andrea, smiled up at him.

"John Sample," she said, "I don't think I've ever seen you look so evil."

In another restaurant, the hostess, without realizing the implication, seated Jeff Richardson, the versatile Jet offensive lineman, at a table next to one occupied by the broad back of Bubba Smith, his former Michigan State roommate.

"See that big man," Richardson whispered to her. "Send him a drink on me, anything he wants, and as many as he wants."

When the hostess informed big Bubba, he turned to look at his benefactor and naturally recognized his college buddy.

"No drinks for me," he said to the hostess. "That man isn't going to get me drinking tonight. No sir, not *tonight*."

Turning to Richardson, he smiled. "But you're going to win tomorrow anyway," he said, sarcastically. "You have the powerhouse. Your quarterback has guaranteed it."

It had begun to rain, and in the Galt lobby, Bake Turner watched the big hard drops bounce off the driveway.

"We don't want rain," he was saying. "Rain will help them more than it will help us. We don't want sun, either, because it can get in a receiver's eyes. What we want is a nice cloudy day, not too hot, not too cool."

During the week, Paul Crane, the quiet member of the Fellowship of Christian Athletes, and Al Atkinson had discussed holding an informal religious service at tomorrow morning's pre-game meal. Players on several other teams, including the Colts, held them. During the season, Crane had thought about it, but never had formulated it. Now, in Crane's room, Atkinson wasn't convinced that tomorrow was the proper time to begin such a service.

"It would be different," the middle linebacker said, "and we haven't done anything different all week."

"Maybe you're right," Crane said, "and if we lose, we might not be able to get the guys to go for it next season. If we have it and lose, they'll be superstitious about it."

On Route A1A, the Iselins were driving through Golden Beach on their way to the Jets' snack. Set among the palm trees on the lawn of Carroll Rosenbloom's home was a big blue-and-white striped tent for the Colts' post-game party.

"Maybe tomorrow night," Phil Iselin said, "he'll wish it were green and white."

In a disciplinary ritual reminiscent of a boarding school or a penitentiary, the eleven p.m. bed-check would be rigidly enforced. The players with wives would not be bothered, but they were expected to be in their rooms. The others would be subject to a knock on the door and inspection from the assistant coaches.

Anyone absent from either would be subject to serious punishment: a $5,000 fine for the Jets, suspension from the game for the Colts.

The $5,000 fine had been instituted several weeks earlier during the Jets' trip to California for games in Oakland and San Diego. The night before the Charger game, Joe Spencer, the offensive line coach, checked the room shared by John Schmitt and Randy Rasmussen, but Schmitt wasn't in sight.

"Where is he?" Spencer asked.

"He told me to tell you that he had to bust out," Rasmussen said.

"That'll cost his ass," Spencer roared.

Suddenly, the bathroom door swung open, and Schmitt emerged, laughing and signalling his presence. At other times, some members of the Jets, like those on all pro football teams, have defied the curfew, mostly during the training-camp weeks when the players begin to tire of the lengthy meetings, the punishing practice sessions, and the jail-like atmosphere.

Of the Jets fined for missing a bed-check during Ewbank's six-season regime, the most celebrated case involved Joe Namath's disappearance prior to a 1967 exhibition game. Another time Rocky Rochester was unable to sleep because of a painfully throbbing injured finger. Hoping to soothe it, he walked the dormitory floor. When the throbbing persisted, he vanished in search of a bottled cure not available in a pharmacy.

The bed-check also inspires frivolity, again involving Rochester, the playful defensive tackle.

On a steamy evening at training camp, Rocky strolled toward the dormitory attired in sandals, bermuda shorts, and a T-shirt. In keeping with such sartorial splendor, he was carrying a black attaché case.

"Open it," ordered one of the coaches.

Inside were six chilled cans of beer.

Occasionally, a player escapes successfully *after* the bed-check. When the Jets were training at the Peekskill Military Academy, they slept in an old ivy-covered, red-brick building. One of their storied athletes, middle linebacker Wahoo McDaniel, decided to descend the ivy from his third-floor window. Halfway down, the ivy snapped.

"He landed in a heap," recalled a teammate, "and it knocked the wind out of him."

But it did not deter him. Gasping for breath, he soon was up and running toward town.

"We could hear him groaning, 'Uhhhh, uhhhhh,' as he ran down the hill for a few beers."

Among the Colts, the most memorable escapade occurred a decade earlier, after a bed-check during a week's stay in California. It was a situation similar to the restrictive one of training camp, and also similar to McDaniel's method. The hotel was being renovated, with scaffolding on the wall outside the windows. The temptation was too much for Alex Hawkins, one of the Colts' freer spirits.

"But when the Hawk got to the bottom of the scaffold," said a teammate, "he was 20 feet above the ground. The workmen had taken away the ladder that had been there during the day."

In his consternation, Hawkins attracted several spectators but he eventually leaped safely into a sand pit. An hour later, the Colt coaches took another bed-check, an occasional manuever. Hawkins's absence was discovered, resulting in the subtraction of $400 from his next paycheck.

No scaffolding and no ivy were on the outside walls of the Galt Ocean Mile and the Statler Hilton. Even if there were, a sentry would not be necessary tonight.

Larry Grantham and his wife, Linda, were driving back from dinner at a friend's home. "I'd even take the loser's share," the linebacker said, "as long as we win tomorrow."

The snack was a Jet ritual the night before a road game. The idea was to attract the players to have something to eat and drink, and then for them to go to their rooms for the 11 p.m. bed-check. During the season, the players had drifted into the small banquet rooms in the AFL cities in groups of two or three, but now, at the Galt, more than 200 players, coaches, club officials, newsmen, wives, relatives, and friends had swarmed in almost at once. The folding partition between the Continental Room and the Imperial Room had been pushed back forming a huge hall.

At the buffet table, the guests were choosing from plates of fried chicken, cold cuts, and a variety of salads. Nearby were bottles of beer, soft drinks, and milk.

Some of the players were attired casually, in turtle-neck shirts and bermuda shorts. Others were more dressed up, some having recently returned from dinner elsewhere. At about 10:30, with the buffet line vanished, Phil Iselin walked to the microphone on the small stage.

"This is just a snack," the president began. "It's not the last supper."

After a laugh, he introduced Perry Botkin, an old friend of Weeb Ewbank. Botkin had a reputation as one of Hollywood's best musical arrangers. He played a couple tunes on his tiny guitar, then Bake Turner, the Jets' own music man, stepped onstage. Plucking his guitar country-style, he sang, "I'm For Love." When he finished, Andre Kostelanetz, the old maestro, slid onto the seat behind the nearby piano. With a flourish, Bake signalled to him and their duet of "Malaguena" produced serious, sincere applause.

"Hey, Bake," somebody called, "you really carried that piano player."

Not everybody was laughing. In a far corner, behind the edge of the folded partition, Matt Snell stared across the room. He was wearing a black sportshirt, black bermudas, and, with his black body in the shadows, the whites of his eyes sparkled fiercely, like two diamonds on black satin.

"Look at Snell's eyes," somebody whispered. "Will you look at his *eyes*."

Moments later, after some brief goodnight words from Iselin and Ewbank, everybody scattered. Not long after that, Joe Spencer strolled through the lobby.

"All my dahlin's are in bed," the assistant coach said. "I guess I can go to bed myself."

Upstairs, on the fifth floor, Clive Rush knocked on the Governor's Suite door. Jim Hudson had moved to another room with his wife, and Joe Namath, stripped to his shorts, answered the knock.

"Have you seen anything new?" Rush said.

"The same stuff," the quarterback said. "It's the same on this reel as it was on the others."

At the snack, Namath had requested a reel of the Colt-Viking game that he hadn't examined before.

"Any questions?" asked Rush.

"I can't think of any now."

Downstairs, in the quiet of the lobby, Ewbank turned to some friends.

"We unwound 'em tonight," the coach said, "and we'll rewind 'em tomorrow."

In the Imperial Room, the tables were being cleared as John Free surveyed the remnants of the snack.

"I've never seen it like this before," the traveling secretary said. "Look at all the food that's left on the plates. Usually there isn't a morsel left. And look over at the beer. They only took about seventy bottles, out of the two hundred we had there. Usually the beer is the first thing to disappear."

Free glanced at Dave Searles, the Galt's convention manager, and nodded knowingly.

"Dave," he said, seriously, "you're looking at the first sign of tomorrow's victory."

Upstairs, Gerry Philbin was under the covers when his wife Trudy folded the gold spread on the other double bed.

"No, no," he said. "Sleep in here. I won't hit you."

During their marriage, the defensive end occasionally has bolted from his sleep in a violent rage, as if he were assaulting a quarterback. Once, in his fury, he slammed his wife in the face, severely bruising her jaw, and clawed at her arms. On this night before the most important football game her husband would play, her precaution was understandable. But not wanting to annoy him, she slid in beside him.

Casually, they talked of the game, but soon she realized that he was asleep, much sooner than he usually is before a game. He often is a restless sleeper, but throughout this night, he would sleep easily. And she would sleep safely.

Winston Hill slept with blood in his eye, a tiny red dot on his left eyeball that had appeared mysteriously a few weeks earlier. Two weeks ago tonight, before the AFL championship game, he had dreamt of Ben Davidson, the mustached Raider defensive end. Davidson was roaring toward him on a motorcycle. But tonight he would not dream of Ordell Braase.

In the darkness, Don Maynard awoke with the realization that the electric heating pad was strapped to his left thigh. Almost subconsciously, he unfastened it, unplugged it, tossed it onto a nearby chair, and quickly went back to sleep. In another room, Bake Turner fluffed the pillow beneath his head and wished he had asked Jeff Snedeker for a sleeping pill.

In the Governor's Suite, the quarterback no longer was alone. Joe Namath had been joined by a casual female acquaintance, and he was enjoying a glass of Johnnie Walker Red. "It's good for you," he would say later about his defiance of the monastic tradition for athletes on the night before the most important game he has played. "It relaxes you."

Dave Herman doesn't smoke cigarets. They make him dizzy. But the night before a game, to induce sleep, he smokes one. It had worked again. He was asleep, his concern over Bubba Smith forgotten. But suddenly, in the darkness, his wife Leah was yanking at his shoulders.

"I don't want you to play," she was sobbing. "It's not right that they make you play out of position."

As he reached out for her, the tears on her cheeks dampened his hands, jolting him into wakefulness.

"If you lose," she was saying now, "all the blame will be dumped on you if Bubba has a big day. All this 'Kill, Bubba, Kill'—what is this game coming to? I don't want to be a widow; oh, I'm so frightened."

Gently, he comforted her. Dave Herman went back to sleep, but his wife wept for hours.

SUNDAY, JANUARY 12
"Sixteen-to-Seven"

The kickoff would be at three o'clock. Weeb Ewbank always schedules his team's pre-game meal four hours before the kickoff. Now, at eleven, the Jets had assembled in the Directors Room of the Galt, its windows streaked with the morning drizzle. On the long tables were pitchers of orange juice and milk, pots of coffee, platters of toast, and jars of honey. Next to each of the plates was a salad bowl. The players could ask for sirloin steak, chopped steak, eggs, or pancakes, whichever they preferred.

As waitresses moved quickly among the tables, the clatter of china interrupted the quiet. Joe Namath sliced his steak and, as he would say later, "forced myself" to swallow a few bites. He also gulped a few spoonfuls of honey. Randy Beverly picked at his salad but ignored everything else. Jim Turner chewed on some steak but had no liquids. Johnny Sample didn't touch a thing.

Ralph Baker munched on his chopped steak and worried that he was too relaxed. Dave Herman stared in silence.

Without a word, Herman and his wife, Leah, had dressed, and he had sat with her in the Bimini Room as she sipped coffee. All around them, other players and other wives had passed by, but he hadn't acknowledged them. Intent on his confrontation with Bubba Smith, he had looked out the big glass windows at rain dripping off the palm trees near the pool. Suddenly, he had stood to join his teammates.

"I'm going to kill him," he had mumbled to his wife. "I'm really going to kill him."

But now, in the Directors Room, the offensive tackle's meditation was interrupted when John Free passed among the players, handing out Super Bowl souvenirs from the Commissioner's office—a tie clasp and a small, round traveling bag.

"They really went all out for us," Namath cracked, holding up the inexpensive tie clasp. "They really went all out."

Some players smiled. Not all. Through a miscalculation, John Free was four bags short. The traveling secretary apologized, and assured the four players they would receive their bags later, but that did not stop them from griping. Another gripe existed, too. The day before, the AFL owners had installed a new playoff system for the 1969 season whereby the first-place team in each division would oppose the second-place team in the other division, with the winners meeting in the championship game.

"Listen to this," snarled Larry Grantham, reading a newspaper, "they put this in: 'To assure the best team of getting to the Super Bowl.' I guess they don't think *we're* the best team."

Across the room, Jeff Snedeker was taping the ankles of most of the players, one by one, as they sat barefoot on a table. Once the team gets to the stadium, the trainer doesn't have enough time to tape ankles. He's too busy taping knees. But now, as most of the players finished whatever they would eat this morning, Ewbank spoke from the coaches' table.

"All right now, let's have your attention," he said. "I want to go over a few things."

The coach reminded them that poise and execution would provide their opportunity for success, and then he explained how he had solved the dilemma of which unit, offensive or defensive, to select for the glamorous pre-game introduction.

"If we win the toss, we'll receive," Ewbank said. "In that case, I want my quarterback warming up, so we'll introduce the defense. If we lose the toss and kickoff, we'll introduce the offense."

Ordinarily, it works the opposite way, but Joe Namath pierced the silence.

"What the hell, Weeb," the quarterback said, "just introduce the seniors."

Now, for the first time, the players laughed. Introducing the seniors is a college custom in the final game of the season, and all the players appreciated the humor of the wisecrack. The tension no longer was quite so oppressive, and when Weeb Ewbank dismissed his players, many of them appeared more relaxed. But as Jim Hudson departed, he grumbled at John Free about the shortage of traveling bags.

"Damn," the safetyman said, "when you screw up, John Free, I always get stuck."

Waiting until Hudson was out of earshot, Free said softly, "I'm glad he's mad."

At the Statler Hilton, the Colts had eaten at the same time as the Jets. The essence of Don Shula's address was his constant theme. "Once again," he reminded his players, "everything that we've accomplished all year is riding on this game."

Weeb Ewbank had returned to his room when the phone rang. One of his old Baltimore friends had requested a few tickets for several priests, and the coach had arranged for them. But now, on the phone, one of the priests had a complaint.

"These tickets are on the 35-yard line," he said.

"That was the best I had left," Ewbank said, "but that's pretty good, you know."

"But you don't understand," the priest continued.

"What is there I don't understand?" Ewbank said.

"Our monsignor is going to use one of these seats, and I can't let the monsignor sit on the 35-yard line. Don't you have anything on the 50-yard line?"

"Father," said the coach, "I couldn't get the Pope a seat on the 50-yard line now."

Outside the Galt, three buses were waiting, but Johnny Sample and his college roommate, Alfa Mouton, walked to a car.

"You drive," Sample said.

Alfa Mouton had been a linebacker at Maryland State when Sample was the team's star. "He played on my side on defense," Sample once said, "and he was tough. He'd yell at the other team, 'Don't run this way! I'm a great tackler!' Then he'd turn to me and say, 'Save yourself for offense, old Alf will do the tackling.' He was a tough cat." But today, old Alf was silent as Sample, alone in the back seat, stared out the windows.

"I didn't say a word the whole trip, not a single word," Sample would say later, "and old Alf was afraid to."

At the Orange Bowl, several policemen hurried past the big white NBC mobile-unit truck into the stadium.

"Follow them," Jim Marooney, the network's unit manager, told one of his aides. "Find out what's wrong."

There had been an anonymous phone call, alerting the police to a bomb scare. The police ordered the stadium closed. When the Miami Police Department's big bomb-disposal truck arrived, it eased to a stop alongside the NBC mobile unit.

"Do me a favor," Marooney said to a police officer. "Park your bomb truck somewhere else."

The mobile unit was stocked with a million dollars worth of equipment to control the national telecast of the game. The police agreed. The bomb-disposal truck was moved to another area. But no bomb was found, and the stadium soon was reopened.

Outside the Galt, the third bus filled quickly with Jet wives and relatives. The first two were for the players. Larry Grantham was among the first to board the second bus. He walked back to the long rear seat and plopped himself in the middle, where he could survey his teammates. Continually, almost compulsively, as if he were hoping it would release the tension within him, the old line-backer was talking to anybody who would listen.

"I got a telegram signed by everybody in my hometown," he was saying. "Had three names on it. . . I woke up at two, and at five-thirty . . . Back here, Don Maynard, plenty of room for your legs . . . Get another bus, John Free, we can't sit around here all day long. Get another bus, let's go."

Several seats ahead, Mark Smolinski, the leader of the special teams, eased next to a window. Moments later, Bill Mathis sat with him.

"I've never seen anything like this," Smo said. "These guys are just waiting to hit somebody."

Soon the buses moved past the people clustered around the hotel entrance and out onto Galt Ocean Drive to wait for the three Colt buses. Now, even Grantham was silent. The only noise was the click of the big windshield wipers. Outside, two motorcycle policemen, in white helmets and brown uniforms, had been assigned to escort the convoy. When the Colt buses arrived from the Statler Hilton, one of the drivers transporting the Jets spoke into his intercom.

"I see we've got the Colts behind us," he said. "Let's keep it that way all day."

The players laughed and with the motorcycle sirens whining, the convoy was on its way down Route A1A, across Sunrise Boulevard, past a roadstand with a sign proclaiming "Spicey Baltimore Deviled Crab," and then past several blocks of low-slung homes to the Sunshine State Parkway. At the toll-gates, the sun had sneaked through the clouds. But soon the clouds blotted out the sun again. Rocky Rochester liked that. The less glare, the less chance his bad eye would produce a headache.

As the buses rumbled along the southbound lane, Joe Namath called over to John Schmitt.

"Do you," he said to the center, smiling, "*really* think you can block these guys?"

Across the aisle, Al Atkinson read *In Cold Blood*. Gerry Philbin stared out the window at the traffic on the northbound lane. Every so often the big defensive end would yawn loudly, like a caged lion. The buses moved onto Interstate 95, and soon they turned off, approaching the Orange Bowl, the rim of the big stadium set against the clouds.

"There it is, baby," Smolinski said. "Here we are."

The streets were snarled with traffic. Up ahead, a drawbridge began to rise above a canal where several party boats were approaching.

"You did it to us again, John Free," yelled a player.

But suddenly, the boats churned to a stop. The drawbridge was lowered for the buses. On the sidewalks, people were waving or hooting at the Jet buses. One youngster was grinning wildly, waving his thumbs down. "Grin, you jackass, grin," snapped Grantham.

Soon the buses eased inside the wire fence of the stadium grounds and through the gantlet of spectators. Peering into the windows, their faces were only a few feet away. At least half of them were carrying an allegiance to the Jets—a green pennant, or a green band on their $2 straw hats. One fat man wore an old T-shirt with "Go, Jets, Go" written on it in ball-point blue.

Eventually, the first bus reached the players' gate. When the door hissed open, a crowd surged around it. One fan shouted, "Namath on this one?" The others also were calling for the quarterback.

"Joe," said Pete Lammons, "you better get off first, or nobody on this bus will make the kickoff."

Namath complied, the spectators yelling to him and reaching out to touch him as he shouldered through them. Behind him, his teammates followed, moving quickly through the crowd and then through the dark tunnel leading to the dressing room on the north side of the field. Soon the second bus was unloading, and as Verlon Biggs got off, he held two tickets that he had been unable to dispose of. Noticing a small boy, he offered them to him. The boy backed away.

"Take 'em," Biggs said. "Two free tickets."

Grabbing them now, the boy ran off, holding them aloft in triumph.

Somehow the third bus, the one with the Jet wives and relatives, had become separated from the convoy. In the traffic jam near the stadium, the driver opened his window to seek directions from a policeman.

"All the Jet wives are on this bus," he said, "and we're lost."

"Not *we*," chorused several wives. "*You* are the one who's lost."

In the Jets' dressing room, each player's number and name had been inked on a strip of white adhesive tape above his wall hook. The "12 Namath" was in the middle of a large printed sign, posted by the league, reminding the competitors not to gamble on games. At intervals along the benches was a Super Bowl program for each player, and after they hung up their clothes, many of them glanced through its pages.

"What the hell," said Jim Hudson, wearing the red shorts his wife had brought from Texas. "This your fault, Frank?"

In a few programs, the season statistics of the Oakland Raiders had been printed instead of the Jet figures.

"I don't handle that," Frank Ramos said. "They prepare for both teams. Somebody goofed, that's all."

"Damn," muttered Hudson. "*We* get in the Super Bowl and the program's got the goddamn Raiders in it."

Next to him. Johnny Sample appeared unaware of Hudson's complaint. His eyes aglow, his face taut, Sample had not yet removed any of his clothes. He prefers to wait until the final few minutes before the warmup and change into his uniform quickly. Ordinarily, he spends this time on the field, looking for spots where he could slip in covering a receiver. But today he remained in the dressing room. Soon, he would enter the tiled shower room. Alone, he would kneel and pray for several minutes. But now he sat on his bench, putting new white laces into his football shoes. Every so often, his cheeks would puff, and he would exhale. Then he would take a deep breath.

Jim Turner disappeared. The place-kicker was in one of the toilet stalls.

In the middle of the long rectangular room, Clive Rush glanced at his watch.

"Kickers and receivers," he announced. "Kickers and receivers out at one-twenty-two, it's one-twenty-seven right now. I mean out at *two*-twenty-two, it's *one*-twenty-seven now."

On the cement floor, George Sauer, Jr., was on his back and holding his ankles.

"I'm pretending I'm a frog layin' on its back," the split end said.

At the far end of the room, Larry Grantham, Rocky Rochester, John Elliott, and Curley Johnson sprawled on the floor, reading their programs silently. Up near the front, Babe Parilli noticed Dr. Nicholas.

"Hey there, Coach Doc, stay loose," Parilli said. "No penalties on the sideline, Doc."

In the trainer's room, Joe Namath stood on the taping table, his right leg bent, the heel slightly raised, his right hand gently holding a thin ceiling pipe. Working skillfully and quickly, Jeff Snedeker applied white adhesive tape above, around, and below the knee to hold the joint in a "slight bit of flexion." That way, the leg would not be fully extended if it should be whacked, hopefully averting additional knee damage. Then he fastened an aluminum-and-black-rubber brace to the knee, taping it securely in place.

When the trainer finished, Namath's right leg was virtually in an adhesive cast.

The quarterback was unable to get down from the table. Several days earlier, as he waited for Snedeker to help him down, he had said, "You ought to have steps here." Now he said nothing as the trainer, holding him around the waist, lowered him to the floor. But for Jeff Snedeker, the taping had only begun. He would tape the knees of nine other players while Namath, clad only in a jockstrap, calmly lathered his face and shaved.

No needles would be necessary in the pre-game preparations. Dave Herman's ankle had improved, and Don Maynard's thigh was rubbed with analgesic balm.

Namath, meanwhile, had returned from shaving. Near him was Reverend Paul Scullin, S.A., a gray-haired Catholic priest from the Graymoor Monastery in Garrison, New York, close to where the Jets once trained.

"What should I pray for, Joe?" the Franciscan friar asked.

"Father," the quarterback said, "pray that nobody gets hurt."

Eventually, when the Jets filed out for their warmup, Ralph Baker stayed close to Namath. For the previous four games, Baker had gone onto the field with him and a cheer went up. "It made me feel," he had said, "like they were cheering for me." But now, when he heard the beginning of the roar for the quarterback, Baker dropped behind.

"I was too embarrassed," he would say later. "I let Joe go down the field by himself."

In reality, not all the noise was cheers. There were sarcastic sneers from spectators who hoped that the boastful quarterback would learn a lesson from the mighty Colts, the impregnable NFL champions. Not that Namath appeared affected by the situation. He moved easily. Perhaps the most tense Jet now was Bake Turner, convinced that he would be the surprise starter at flanker. "My stomach was light and empty, but not nauseous," he would confess. He thought how much different he had felt as he waited offstage before appearing on *The Ed Sullivan Show*.

"Playing a guitar and singing," he would say, "the chance of making a mistake is almost none. But in football, you can fumble or drop a pass, and everybody knows it."

Meanwhile, the actual coin toss was about to occur at midfield, half an hour before the kickoff. Joe Namath was one of the Jet captains, but he was busy throwing passes. So Johnny Sample, the captain of the defensive unit, joined the game referee, Tommy Bell of the NFL staff, and one of the Colt captains, Lenny Lyles.

"You don't have to introduce us," Sample said, glancing at his long-time buddy.

"All right, Captain Sample," said Bell, "the Jets have been designated as the visiting team. Wait until the coin is in the air and call it loud."

As the referee flipped a silver dollar toward the cloudy sky, Sample called, "Heads" and watched the big coin spin onto the rain-softened grass.

"Heads it is," Bell announced.

The Jets would receive, and Sample smiled. "The first one," he said to Lyles, "goes to us."

Weeb Ewbank was returning to the Jet locker room when he was approached by Carroll Rosenbloom, the Colt owner.

"We're having a party tonight at my home in Golden Beach," said Rosenbloom, "and we'd like to have you and Lucy come by."

The old coach, once discharged by Rosenbloom, smiled. "I appreciate it, Carroll," he said, "but we won't be able to make it."

Ewbank called Don Maynard and Bake Turner into his office where Clive Rush and Dr. Nicholas joined them.

"How'd your leg feel out there?" Ewbank asked.

"I'll be all right," Maynard said. "It's not 100 percent, but I'll be all right."

"Will it hold up?" Ewbank asked the doctor.

"It should. He's given it a good rest here."

"I've got complete faith in Bake," the coach resumed, turning to Maynard, "and I'd rather have a healthy man there."

"Coach," Maynard said, "I'll be all right."

"All right," the coach decided, "but if it goes on you, don't hide it."

"If it goes," Maynard said, "you'll see it."

Turner was surprised. He had assumed that he would start, but now Ewbank turned to him.

"Be ready," the coach said. "Be watching."

Turner knew that if Maynard pulled up lame, he would replace him immediately. But if Ewbank had to lose a regular on the offensive unit, he believed that the drop in efficiency from Maynard to Turner at flanker was perhaps less than at any position.

In their room, the Colts were listening to Don Shula's words. "Don't wait for the Jets to lose it," the coach warned. "We've got to win it ourselves."

The Jets also were listening. The silence in their room had been pierced by Weeb Ewbank's voice.

"Some of you men," the coach was saying, "used to be with the Colts, but that team decided that you didn't have the skills to stay with them. Now you're *opposing* that team. You've proven to yourself that you're capable. Now you've got an opportunity to prove it to *that* team."

He turned to Randy Rasmussen, the young guard from little Kearney State, his face grim with anticipation.

"And you, Randy, you've got a chance to prove that a player from a small college belongs in the Super Bowl."

"You get fifteen thousand dollars for proving it," John Schmitt said softly. "Fifteen thousand dollars."

"Did you see," Ewbank continued, "where Biletnikoff said the wrong AFL team was in this game? The next time anybody sees him, ask him if he meant Kansas City."

Biletnikoff played for Oakland, which defeated Kansas City in a playoff for the AFL's Western Division title.

"Fifteen thousand dollars," Schmitt repeated quietly. "Fifteen thousand dollars is out there for each of us."

"And remember this," the coach went on. "The pressure is not on us. It's definitely on the Colts. But no matter what develops out there, I expect you to maintain your poise and your execution. That's what we've worked on all season, and that's why we're here. All right, let's have our prayer now."

As usual, Paul Crane led the team prayer while each player knelt and joined hands with the teammates on each side of him.

"I'll always remember that moment," Crane would say later. "Our fellowship together as a team was very precious at that moment, a team that humbled itself before God."

After the recitation of The Lord's Prayer, the coach held up his hands to say something else.

"One more thing," Ewbank said "When we win, don't pick me up and ruin my other hip. I'll walk."

With a laugh, the forty players stood and, their white helmets in their hands, their cleats clattering on the cement floor, they filed out the wide door beneath the end-zone stands. When the first few players appeared at the edge of the field, the noise began to come down around them. The noise of cheers was mixed with the noise of jeers, causing a loud rumble. As the coaches and most players moved toward the sideline bench, the eleven members of the starting defensive unit waited to be introduced.

"Get in the proper order now," said John Free, "and don't leave until you hear your number."

Usually, the players teased the traveling secretary as they awaited their introductions, but today they silently fell into line. *They're organized*, Free thought, *they're really organized to follow the game plan*. One by one, with the announcement of their number over the public-address system as their cue, they ran out near the goal posts before veering off to the sideline.

Behind the bench, Joe Namath had been warming up, drilling short passes.

"My arm feels so loose," he said, joining his teammates near the sideline. "I think it's going to fall off."

Hearing him, John Dockery glanced at the quarterback's dangling right arm.

"Standing there in the breeze," the Harvard man would say later, "his arm really did seem to shake oddly."

Nearby, Weeb Ewbank, wearing a gray suit and his white baseball cap with the green peak, was unsure of his decision to open with Don Maynard.

"Do you think his leg will really hold up?" he was asking Dr. Nicholas.

"Start him and see what happens," the doctor suggested. "The Colts don't know he hasn't practiced. See how they defense him. If you don't start him, they'll know something's wrong with him."

"Yeah," said the coach, "if he's there, their defense will have to honor him."

Along the sideline, Curley Johnson watched the kickoff-return unit trot onto the field.

"Chicken ain't nothin' but a bird," the punter shouted. "Chicken ain't nothin' but a bird."

Up in the stands, a man from Baltimore was sitting in the row behind several of the Jet wives.

"The Big Boys," the man from Baltimore was saying, "are going to show the Little Boys how."

Out on the field, the Jets were deployed at intervals for the kickoff and now, as referee Bell's arm came down and his whistle blew,

Lou Michaels moved toward the teed-up football. Synchronized slightly behind him, a line of ten white helmets and blue jerseys advanced. With the thud of the kickoff, the game began. Almost instantly, as the ball soared out of the cloudy sky into Earl Christy's arms 2 yards deep in the end zone, colliding equipment clacked. For the members of the Jet kickoff unit, the films had a familiar sound track now as several Colts converged on Christy at the 23-yard line and brought him down.

Moments later, the Jet offensive unit spun out of its huddle, with Joe Namath slouching over John Schmitt.

Barking signals, Namath called for the shift that provides the Jets with an unbalanced line. Bob Talamini, the left guard, moved over between Schmitt and Randy Rasmussen, the right guard. Talamini now was across from Billy Ray Smith, whose eyes were flashing behind his face mask. At the snap, the Jet line charged forward, with Talamini slamming into Smith as Matt Snell took the handoff and blasted 3 yards. As the players unpiled, Billy Ray glanced at Talamini.

"Congratulations," the Colt tackle said. On the next play, Snell bolted behind Winston Hill, the left tackle, for 9 yards until he was stopped by Rick Volk. But the Colt safetyman did not arise. In tackling Snell, he had lowered his head too far. The impact jarred him. His mind reeling, his legs wobbly, he had to be helped to the sideline. Matt Snell had established the Jet running game.

At the moment, though, the Jets were unable to advance beyond their own 40, and Curley Johnson came in to punt. Early in his career, his hands were wet with sweat when he waited for the ball. He had wondered if they would be sweaty today. They were not.

Now the Colts were starting at their own 27, and on the first play, Earl Morrall passed over the middle to John Mackey for a 19-yard gain that appeared to destroy all the Jet preparations for the tight end. In the coaches' booth, Walt Michaels shouted into the phone to Mike Stromberg.

"Grantham took his eye off Mackey," the coach boomed. "The linebackers have to help on him. They have to help."

On the next play, halfback Tom Matte swept for 10 more yards. Jerry Hill got 7, Matte got 1, then Hill slammed for 5 more yards and a third first down at the Jet 31.

"What the hell is going on?" growled a voice in the Jet defensive huddle. "Let's start doing something."

Gerry Philbin did. On the next play, he got past Sam Ball and stopped Hill for a 3-yard loss. Morrall under-threw a pass to Jimmy Orr, but on third-and-13, with Tom Mitchell inserted as an extra tight end, Morrall found Orr for a 15-yard gain. First down on the Jet 19. But after two incompletions, Morrall was tackled at the scrimmage line as he scrambled up the middle.

The Colts had been stopped, but with Michaels kicking from the 27, a field goal seemed likely. He missed.

The Jets had a reprieve. Now the Jets had their chance. After a 13-yard pass to Bill Mathis for a first down at the Jet 35, Namath dispatched Maynard down the sideline. His white shoes moving backward like two cottontail rabbits, Namath heaved the ball as Maynard broke beyond Jerry Logan, the safetyman in the Colt zone defense. But the long pass tipped Maynard's outstretched fingers. The flanker had been a stride short.

"Damn," said Ewbank, second-guessing himself. "If his leg's right, that's a touchdown."

When the flanker later returned to the bench, he informed Dr. Nicholas that he had "felt" a twinge in his thigh on the deep sideline pattern but that he could continue. Ewbank thought about inserting Turner, but decided against it because the Colts were rotating their zone defense toward Maynard, and that would enable George Sauer to operate against Lyles in more one-on-one situations. To throw to Sauer, however, Namath would have to throw to his left, and he was having trouble doing that.

"For some reason," the quarterback told Sauer on the sideline, "my thumb bothers me when I throw to the left."

After the long pass off Maynard's fingers, he had missed Sauer in a third-and-4 situation at the Jet 41, prompting another Johnson punt. But this time, despite good field position at their 45, the Colt offense sputtered. Mackey dropped a pass. Hill made 3. On third-and-7, Morrall threw toward Willie Richardson, but Johnny Sample batted it away without a word. In his emotional frenzy, Sample had been uncharacteristically quiet.

Pinned on the Jet 4 by a punt, Namath used Snell for 4 and 5 yards. On third-and-1, the quarterback drilled a quick pass to Sauer.

But as Sauer caught the ball, apparently for a first down, he was slammed in the back by Lyles and fumbled. The loose ball was pounced upon at the 12 by Ron Porter, who had temporarily replaced Don Shinnick at right linebacker. It was the first break of the game, and as Sauer trotted glumly across to the Jet bench, the Colts appeared sure to score.

"All right now," Ewbank was shouting at the defensive unit, "keep your poise, keep your poise."

Sauer plopped onto the bench where he tried to hide from his teammates. His father attempted to relax him.

"It's early," his father said. "You know what you can do."

Moments later, Winston Hill walked near the split end.

"Thank you, George," the big tackle said to the end who seldom fumbled. "You showed me you were human."

At that, Sauer lifted his head and returned the smile.

Meanwhile, the Jet defense was maintaining its poise. On first down, Philbin had smeared Hill for a 1-yard loss. Opening the second quarter, Matte had gained 7 yards on a sweep to the 6. If the Jets could prevent a touchdown or a first down, they would force the Colts to settle for a field goal. As middle linebacker Al Atkinson watched Morrall move up to the line of scrimmage, he hunched his left shoulder. In the pileup on the previous play, the shoulder had been jammed. Now, at the snap, Morrall spun to his left and Atkinson moved that way.

Behind the middle linebacker, Tom Mitchell had eluded Randy Beverly and was free in the end zone. Morrall threw, but Atkinson, leaping high with his right hand extended, grazed the ball. Its spiral was affected. So was its direction. The ball veered higher and behind Mitchell, landing on his shoulder pads and bounding into the air above Beverly, who caught it in the end zone for a touchback.

"I tipped the ball with my right hand," Atkinson would say, "but I couldn't have raised my left hand that high."

Instead of a Colt touchdown or field goal, the touchback enabled the Jets to take over on their 20-yard line. Sauer's fumble had been erased by Beverly's interception. Poise had been maintained and execution would be provided. Snell moved the Jets to their 46 in four consecutive running plays aimed at the right side of the Colt defense, where linebacker Shinnick was unable to avoid halfback Emerson Boozer's blocks.

"Follow me," Boozer was saying to Snell in the huddle. "I'm splitting him down the middle."

Namath wasn't saying much in the huddle. Because of the constantly shifting Colt defense, the quarterback often had used an "automatic," meaning a new play called at the line of scrimmage. He decided now that rather than change the play, he simply would call it at the line of scrimmage after he had surveyed the Colt defense.

"Play at the line," he would say in the huddle. "Check with me."

Namath's upper lip curled above his teeth as he shouted the code of colors, letters, and numbers that his teammates deciphered instantly. After another wild pass to Sauer on the left side, Namath defied a safety blitz with a quick pass to Mathis for 6 yards into Colt territory. Confronted with a critical third-and-4 situation, he whipped a pass to Sauer for a 14-yard gain and a first down at the 34. On the next play, with Sauer running a square-out pattern to the sideline, the quarterback risked another pass to his left. Lyles lunged for the ball, but it zipped past his hands and into Sauer's hands for an 11-yard gain and a first down at the 23.

"I was lucky on that one," Namath would say. "Because if Lyles picks it off, he's got a touchdown."

"Lyles mistimed it," another Jet said, "because nobody in the NFL throws that pass that fast."

With the Colt defense undershifted, Boozer plunged behind Randy Rasmussen for 2 yards. On second down, Namath tossed a flare pass to Snell, and the fullback galloped 12 yards through an area unprotected by left linebacker Mike Curtis, who had moved out to help cornerback Bobby Boyd cover Maynard.

"What are you doin' out here?" Maynard said to Curtis as they returned to their respective huddles. "That was your coverage."

On first down at the 9, Snell blasted behind Rasmussen to the 4, and when the Colts unpiled, they were growling.

"I could hear them cursing to themselves in their huddle," John Schmitt would say. "They were frustrated by our drive."

In their frustration, the Colts realized that the Jets had not been intimidated by their NFL reputation. In one of the pileups, Schmitt's stomach was being pounded by Billy Ray Smith's fists.

"You do that again," Schmitt snapped, "and you won't get up."

Smith snapped back, but respect had been achieved in the trenches, where football games are won. Most of the time, Schmitt was involved in blocking middle linebacker Dennis Gaubatz. According to Claude (Buddy) Young, the one-time Colt halfback, he would "play the best game I've ever seen a center play." Next to him, Rasmussen was jolting Billy Ray Smith, and Dave Herman was neutralizing big Bubba Smith. Mike Curtis, "the Animal," had been caged by tight end Pete Lammons. Meanwhile, the left side of the Jet line had protected the quarterback and the runners as if they were jewels on display. In appraising the Colt defense, Bob Talamini had commented that "they try to confuse you." But Fred Miller wasn't confusing him. Even more important in the psychological struggle, Winston Hill discovered that Ordell Braase had aged considerably since that haunting 1963 training camp.

Braase, his back aching, had to be rested occasionally, and his replacement, Lou Michaels, wasn't doing much.

Now, as Joe Namath surveyed the situation with a second down on the 4, he chose the play known as the "19 Option"—a handoff to Snell to the left side. At the snap, Hill and Talamini jammed their men, and Boozer chopped down Rick Volk, the safetyman who had returned from his earlier collision with Snell. Sprung to the outside, Snell muscled by Gaubatz and bounced into the end zone.

Jim Turner's conversion was good, and the Jets had a 7–0 lead.

For the first time in the brief history of the Super Bowl, the AFL representative was ahead. Throughout the double-decked stadium, noise cascaded down at the Jets. In the row behind the Jet wives, the man from Baltimore shrugged.

"The Big Boys," he said, "are letting the Little Boys have their fun."

"The Little Boys," one of the wives snapped back, "are doing all right."

After the kickoff, the Colt offense stalled. Trying for a field goal from the 46, Michaels missed again. But after Turner missed a field goal from the 41, the Colts began to move. Morrall hit Richardson for a 6-yard gain. On second down, Tom Matte smashed through Jim Hudson's arms at the line and broke into the clear along the right sideline. Angling from across the field, Bill Baird bounced him out of bounds at the Jet 16 as Johnny Sample joined the pileup.

"You're a dirty player," Matte flared at Sample.

"And you're a bush-leaguer," Sample snapped, jaw to jaw. "Anybody who gets that far out in front and can't score, no need to play at all."

"Get away, John," Baird yelled, grabbing his teammate. The debate ended. But after Hill gained a yard, Morrall threw toward

Richardson near the goal posts. Sample darted in front of the flanker, intercepting the pass and tumbling at the 2-yard line. As he arose, he tapped the ball against Richardson's white helmet.

"This is what you're lookin' for," Sample said. Richardson burned silently. His introduction to Sample, which Lyles had attempted to perform a week ago, had occurred several plays earlier. In a defensive switch, Sample was covering Jimmy Orr and flattened the little split end as he came off the line. Richardson sought out the Jet cornerback.

"You hit me like that," the flanker said, "and I'll kill you."

At his next opportunity, Sample whacked Richardson, the impact jarring his white Colt helmet from his head.

"All right," Sample said, "you got your chance to kill me."

Now, following the interception, Sample danced toward the Jet bench while Richardson, his head low, trotted to the other sideline. Another scoring opportunity had been wasted. But after an end-zone punt by Curley Johnson, the Colts took over at the Jet 42 with 43 seconds remaining in the half. With a sudden realignment of linebackers in the Jet defense, Larry Grantham was in the middle, replacing Atkinson, and Paul Crane was on the right. Atkinson's bruised shoulder had been severely damaged in the previous series, and he was walking to the dressing room.

"Get inside right now," Dr. Nicholas had told him, "so I'll have more time to fix you up between halves."

Crane stopped Hill after a 1-yard gain on a short pass, and with 25 seconds showing on the scoreboard clock, Morrall sent Matte toward the right side of the Colt line. But suddenly, Matte turned and lateraled to Morrall as Orr floated free beyond Beverly along the sideline near the end zone. Morrall had collaborated with Orr on the same play, known as the flea-flicker, for a 46-yard touchdown pass against the Atlanta Falcons in the second game of their NFL schedule. But now, with Orr wide open and waving his arms, Morrall threw toward Hill in front of the goal posts.

"I never saw Jimmy," said Morrall later. "I saw Hill in the clear down the middle."

"The play is designed for Orr," said Shula later. "Morrall's supposed to look for him."

At the moment Morrall threw toward Hill, the fullback was open. But when the ball reached there, Jim Hudson intercepted at the 12. In viewing the films later, Weeb Ewbank contended that if Morrall had thrown to Orr, safety-man Baird might have been able to get back to knock down the pass.

The half ended with the Jets leading, 7–0. Three interceptions had sabotaged Colt touchdown opportunities, and Michaels had missed two field-goal attempts. Heads down, cleats kicking dust, the Colts filed toward their dressing room.

In his hospital room, Jimmy "The Greek" Snyder stared at his television set. "This," he said to a nurse, "is going to be one of those days."

Up in the stands, Frank Borman turned to Don Klosterman. the Houston Oiler general manager. "The Jets," the astronaut said, "really are poised."

In their dressing room, the Jets sat in groups. Clive Rush spoke to the offense, Walt Michaels to the defense. But one of the regulars was missing. Al Atkinson was sitting on the rubbing table in the trainer's room as Dr. Nicholas examined his left shoulder.

"You've got a bad bruise there," the doctor said.

"Don't tell the coaches," the middle linebacker said. "Don't let them know."

"Why not?"

"They don't have anybody else to put in the middle. Don't let them know."

"I'll shoot it," the doctor said.

Atkinson was the only true middle linebacker on the squad. Early in the season, Mike Stromberg had played there when Atkinson had a bruised knee. Stromberg later required knee surgery, leaving the Jets without an adequate replacement. And now, Atkinson looked away as the syringe of Xylecaine emptied through the needle in his shoulder.

"All right," the doctor said to Jeff Snedeker, "tape his pads to the skin."

Outside, the other defensive players were listening to Michaels's adjustments.

"Force 'em to the inside more," he was saying. "Let's space the ends a little wider."

In the offensive group, George Sauer, Jr., was gulping his second Coke of the intermission. The split end had returned to the dressing room "more tired," he would say later, "than I've ever been in my life, really exhausted." He had thought that the change of climate affected him, but then he realized that he had been in Florida for ten days.

"It was just a matter," he says, "of burning up nervous energy."

The second half was about to begin. Sauer had a new supply of nervous energy for his battle with the enormity of it all. Al Atkinson emerged from the trainer's room, his left shoulder numbed.

Across the field, the Colts were annoyed at themselves for not providing the big plays that could have produced as much as 27 points. Don Shula had decided to give Morrall "one series" to accomplish something. If nothing materialized, Johnny Unitas would take over at quarterback.

On the kickoff, Curley Johnson boomed the ball to Timmy Brown at the goal line, and Mark Smolinski stopped him at the 25. On first down, Tom Matte slashed off right tackle, but the impact of Rocky Rochester's tackle produced a fumble. Ralph Baker, the left linebacker, pounced on the loose ball at the 33. Not only had the Jets taken over in scoring position, but the first-down fumble had disrupted Shula's plans. Now he had to give Morrall another series.

In five plays, Namath directed the Jet offense to the 11, but suddenly, the Colt defense stiffened.

Emerson Boozer attempted to sweep left end, but Lenny Lyles moved up to nail him for a 5-yard loss. With second-and-15, Namath was backpedaling when he heard Dave Herman shout, "Look out."

"I knew," the quarterback would say later, "that Bubba was loose."

With his towering strength, Bubba Smith had slammed past Herman, and he was swooping toward Namath. True to his promise on the studio tape the previous Wednesday, big Bubba aimed his 295-pound bulk at the quarterback's upper body, not his knees, grabbing him around the waist and cleanly slamming him to the turf.

"Good play," Namath told Smith as they untangled.

It was a jarring play, too, perhaps more than Namath realized. With third-and-24, he spotted Lammons over the middle, but his pass was nearly intercepted by Jerry Logan. When the ball bounced off his hands, the safetyman threw up his arms in disgust. Another opportunity for a big play by the Colts had been wasted. From the sideline, Jim Turner trotted out for a field-goal attempt as Babe Parilli scraped a mark at the 32-yard line.

"Bow your neck, Tank," yelled Curley Johnson.

Head down, his right hand behind him, Turner swung his square-toed shoe, and the ball, spinning end over end, floated high between the uprights to give the Jets a 10–0 lead.

When the Colts got the ball after the kickoff, Morrall was still at quarterback. But he overthrew Mackey, got no yardage on a short pass to Hill, and lost 2 yards when he was chased out of the pocket. Morrall walked to the sideline, where Unitas, annoyed and impatient, had been warming up his tender elbow.

Soon the Jets had another field goal, from the 30, for a 13–0 lead. But they also had a scare.

Two plays before the field goal, Namath had been whacked on

his sore thumb by Miller and, wringing his hand and holding the thumb, he had raced to the sideline as Parilli replaced him.

"How bad is it, how bad?" asked Ewbank.

"Is it dislocated?" asked Dr. Nicholas. "Let me see it."

"It's just jammed," the quarterback said.

Moments later, Namath was behind the bench, zipping passes. His thumb had recovered. But in the mounting excitement, Weeb Ewbank's mind had not. Out on the field, Johnny Unitas, in his blue jersey with the white "19" and in his ankle-high black shoes, was crouched over the center, his white helmet with the blue horseshoe swinging from side to side as he called signals, the way he had done it for Ewbank for seven seasons. Seeing him again, the old coach forgot himself.

"No interceptions now, John," he mumbled.

At a quick glance, Unitas did look the same. But his right arm wasn't the same. With him unable to throw long, the Jets could stack their defenses against short passes. After a 5-yard run by Matte, the 35-year-old crew-cut quarterback tossed a short pass to Matte for no gain. On third down, his pass to Orr was incomplete. On fourth down, the Colts punted in what would be their last play of the third quarter.

In that period, the Colt offensive unit was on the field for seven plays for a net gain of 10 yards.

"We didn't come down," Rocky Rochester had said, "to make a good showing for the AFL, we came to win."

To the astonishment of the 75,377 spectators and a television audience of perhaps sixty million, the Jets were winning. They had scored 13 points, but primarily, they were winning with defense because the Colts hadn't scored. Three interceptions—two precisely executed, the other lucky—had stopped the Colts in the first half. In the third quarter, though, the Jet defense had dominated completely, despite using a middle linebacker with a stiff left arm. Up front, Philbin and John Elliott had pressured the passer. But the keynote speech had been made by Larry Grantham, the 202-pound linebacker. On an early play, Jerry Hill had blocked Grantham. When they arose, the Colt fullback glanced at him.

"Good hit," Hill said, pleasantly.

"Kiss mine," Grantham responded.

Now, with Namath's thumb well enough for him to return to quarterback, the Jets were about to produce their third field goal. With third-and-7 at the Jet 40, Namath whipped a pass to Sauer on a slant-in pattern, the one they thought would be available in the films. The 11-yard gain provided a first down at the Colt 49.

"Let me fake the slant-in and go," Sauer suggested in the huddle.

"You got it, George," the quarterback said. "Fake it and take off."

At the snap, Sauer took Lyles with him to the inside, then bolted downfield. Namath floated the pass into his hands for a 39-yard gain to the 10. On the next play, Snell got 4 yards behind Herman's block, ending the quarter. As the players walked to the other end of the field, Lyles turned to Sauer.

"I needed some help from my safety on that play," the cornerback said, meaning the long pass. "I don't know where he was."

His safetyman was Rick Volk, who had been severely jolted by Snell on the second play of the game. Volk had returned, but Shula would concede later that the safety-man "had a few lapses out there." One lapse had occurred on that pass to Sauer, the Jets' longest gain. In the Colt zone defense, Volk was to assist Lyles, but the safetyman had missed his assignment.

Namath, meanwhile, had stopped in front of the Jet bench to check his plans with Ewbank.

"I'm not going to take any chances," the quarterback said, thinking of the second-and-6 situation at the 6. "I'm just going to get on the board. You agree with that?"

The coach agreed. Another field goal would make it 16–0, more than two touchdowns ahead.

Snell and Bill Mathis were unable to get the touchdown on line smashes, but no risks had been taken. Turner booted another field goal, this time at a sharp angle from the 9.

There was 13:10 left on the clock as Johnny Unitas, his icy-blue eyes flashing above his face-bar, moved into the huddle after the kickoff. And now, swinging the right arm that had thrown 254 touchdown passes in his NFL career, Johnny Unitas began to do what he was famous for— moving the Colts. On first down from his own 32, he connected with Mackey for 5 yards, then he sent Matte around right end for 7.

With a first down, Unitas drilled a sideline pass to Richardson, who hopped out of bounds at the Colt 44 after a 5-yard gain.

Johnny Sample, a step or two away from Richardson, barrelled into a cluster of Colts in front of their bench. But before the corner-back could escape from the enemy camp, Tom Mitchell, the extra tight end who had not been in the immediate vicinity, moved up the sideline and swung his empty helmet, clunking Sample's helmet. Sample flared, but he wisely hurried back onto the playing field.

"You tell your guys to cut that out," the cornerback yelled at Don Shula. "I'll get Mitchell the next time he comes out here."

Several of the Jets were around Sample now, moving him away from the sideline. Across the field, Ewbank was concerned about his volatile cornerback being in a scuffle. The coach had remembered how Sample, in his crusade against the NFL, had been ejected early in the Jets' first inter-league exhibition with the Philadelphia Eagles in 1967, and he did not want to lose him now. Sample soon calmed, although he could not understand why a penalty wasn't called against Mitchell for such a flagrant swing.

Moments later, Matte ripped off 19 yards for a first down on the Jet 37, then Hill slashed for 12 and another first down at the 25.

On the next play, Richardson streaked at Sample, and Unitas missed him. But Jimmy Orr was not concerned. As the little split end leaned into the huddle, his confidence had been restored. Listening to Johnny U's firm voice, Orr believed that the Colts were going to win, that *somehow* Johnny U would find a way to win, as he had so often.

Now, on second down, Orr burst toward the end zone, and when he turned, Johnny U's pass was floating toward him.

But it was *floating*, not zipping. Randy Beverly cruised in front of Orr and intercepted for another touchback. Not far away, Sample leaped and slapped the back of Matte's helmet.

"It looks bad, buddy," the cornerback shouted.

In his frustration, Matte spun and raced toward Sample, who was trotting toward the Jet bench. Somehow sensing that Matte was after him, the cornerback turned. Before a scuffle could develop, the officials were between them. But when Sample approached the bench, Ewbank confronted him.

"What did you do over at their bench?" the coach demanded.

"I didn't do nothing, Weeb," he piped. "Mitchell hit me with his helmet, Mitchell hit *me*, I didn't do nothing."

"Calm down now."

"I didn't do nothing, I didn't do nothing."

"Don't get upset," the coach said.

"I'm not upset," Sample insisted.

Out on the field, Namath was calling running plays to use as much time as possible. And when Jim Turner missed a 42-yard field goal, the scoreboard clock flashed 6:34—not much time, not even for Johnny Unitas at his best. When Unitas misfired on three consecutive passes, the Colts appeared doomed at their own 20. But on fourth down, he found Orr for 17 yards and a first down. With third-and-10, he hit Mackey for 11. He connected with Richardson for 21, and he found Orr again for 11.

Eventually, the Colts scored when Hill smashed across from the 1—although the Jet defense had held on one play from the 2, and two from the 1.

Only 3:19 remained. Certainly, the Colts would attempt a short kickoff, hoping to recover it. The Jets inserted some of their most sure-handed players, but Michaels's spinning kick squirted away from George Sauer, and Tom Mitchell recovered for the Colts at the Jet 44. In the pileup, Rick Volk was knocked groggy again. To avoid a time out, his teammates dragged him to the nearby sideline.

'Three minutes," Larry Grantham was saying in the huddle now. "That's $5,000 a minute."

Grantham assumed that Unitas would be passing on every play to make the most of the three minutes. The defensive signal-caller's strategy was obvious: permit the short gain in order to prevent the long gain. Unitas accepted the short gain, hitting Richardson for 6 yards, Orr for 14, then Richardson for 5 more. During this sequence, Matte neared the Jet bench, and Mike Martin, the owner's son who had picked up the barbecue tab, hooted him.

"Don't do that," Joe Namath corrected him. "If we're going to be champions, we have to act like champions. They didn't write what was in the papers. They're trying as hard as they can."

The Colts were trying because they conceivably could still win with a quick touchdown, another recovered kickoff, and a field goal. Unitas had performed that magic before. But now, at the 19, he mis-fired on both second down and third down. Confronted with a des-perate fourth-and-5 situation, he threw toward Orr. But Grantham, racing back to help Beverly, reached up and tipped the pass beyond the little split end. In a gesture of triumph, the linebacker who was considered too small to compete in the NFL, took off his helmet and tossed it high.

"And then I realized," he would say later, "that the game wasn't over, and I walked off meekly."

Exactly 2:21 remained, but Matt Snell would preserve the 16–7 victory by carrying on six consecutive plays. By the time the Colts got the ball again, after Curley Johnson's punt, only eight seconds remained. On the Jet sideline, John Free stared sentimentally at Johnny Unitas, whom he had known so well in Baltimore during the quarterback's glory years.

"Look at Unitas out there," said the traveling secretary, "I can't help but feel sorry for him."

"Don't feel sorry for him," Snell snapped. "If we'd lost, he wouldn't be feeling sorry for you."

Underneath the stands, Phil Iselin was hurrying to his team's dressing room. Throughout the final quarter, the Jet president, in his nervousness, had been seeking reassurance from those sitting with him that his players would hold their lead. Now, in the midst of the roar at the final gun, spectators began to spill down the exit near him.

"Is it over?" Iselin called.

"Yes," one of the spectators replied. "It's all over."

"Who won?" Iselin asked.

At his side, Jimmy Iselin stared in disbelief at his father.

Weeb Ewbank knew who won. He was moving across the field to shake hands with Don Shula, the coach who had replaced him in Baltimore, and when they met, Ewbank spoke first.

"We had all the breaks," Weeb said.

"Your team played well," Shula said.

Quickly, they parted, but later, Shula, reflecting on Ewbank's graciousness, would say, "I thought that was pretty nice of him to say that."

Now, on the field, not far from the coaches, Don Shinnick shook hands with Joe Namath.

"Congratulations," said the Colt linebacker, a member of the Fellowship of Christian Athletes, "but always remember the Lord."

Namath nodded. "Thank you," he said. "Good game, and I'll remember that."

Thrusting his right index finger toward the dark sky, signifying that the Jets were the number one team in pro football, the quarterback hurried toward the dressing room. Wagging his finger triumphantly, he disappeared underneath the stands. There, under glaring lights, a television camera was showing the astounded viewers the sweaty, grimy, but happy faces of the world champions.

Jumping and dancing, Dave Herman was one of the first Jets to reach the dressing room.

"Bubba," he roared, releasing his anxieties about the ogre of the Colts whom he had blocked so effectively. "I guess I showed Bubba, I guess I did, I guess I showed big Bubba."

Behind him, his teammates, shouting and smiling, quickly filled the room.

"This is the happiest day of my life," Gerry Philbin shouted. "The happiest day ever."

When all the players were inside, the door was shut, and Weeb Ewbank signalled for silence. "Let's have our prayer," the coach said, nodding toward Paul Crane. Solemnly, with the two captains, Joe Namath and Johnny Sample, holding hands, the players knelt in thanksgiving. When the prayer ended, Ewbank surveyed his team.

"Poise and execution," he said. "That's what we knew we had to have, and that's what we had."

With a whoop, the celebration resumed. The next order of business was awarding the game ball, the symbol of triumph.

"The game ball," Sample announced, "the game ball is going to the league, to the AFL office."

Another cheer. But privacy was about to end. Ewbank told Harold Rosenthal, the AFL information director, that the newsmen, who had been waiting impatiently, could enter. As they poured in, most of them immediately surrounded the quarterback who had *guaranteed* the result.

"I only want to talk to the New York writers," Namath snapped. "They're the only ones who thought we could win."

His reaction typified the emotional involvement of all the Jets—annoyed at their role as an 18-point underdog, annoyed at the insulting newspaper and magazine stories, annoyed at the theory that because they represented an AFL team, they were inferior to players on an NFL team.

"Hey, there's my Dad," the quarterback was saying now. "Let him in here."

Wearing a tilted straw hat with a green Jets band that he had bought for $2 at a concession stand, John Namath eased through the newsmen and embraced his son. Near them, Bob Namath, also wearing one of the straw hats, waited to congratulate his kid brother.

"What a wonderful game," his father said.

"Yeah," the quarterback said, grinning, "but you weren't the one who had to play in it."

"You showed me a winner," his brother said.

"We showed a whole lot of people they were wrong," the quarterback said. "Eighteen-point underdogs. Beautiful."

Emotionally, all the Jets were unwinding.

Matt Snell, who had been "looking to punish people" during the game, was punishing some newsmen now.

"Don't talk to us," he said. "All you wrote was how great Matte and Hill are. Go talk to them now."

Another newsman asked Gerry Philbin if he were surprised.

"Yeah," he answered, "I'm surprised that they scored on us."

Randy Rasmussen, who didn't want to confront Billy Ray Smith at the television studio because "seeing him might scare me out," talked about how he had handled the Colt tackle.

"All the guys he faced in the NFL this year backed off and tried to guess what he'd do," the young guard said. "I stepped up and put it to him. I whipped him pretty good."

Bill Baird, the safetyman who had been cut by the Colts in 1963, appeared calm.

"I wasn't awed by them," he said. "I didn't go in thinking they're great."

The other Colt reject in 1963 who had developed into a Jet

starter, Winston Hill, suddenly was willing to talk about the "unpleas-ant" memory that he had claimed to have crossed out of his mind. Ordell Braase had chased him out of that training camp. But today, Hill had chased Braase out of the Super Bowl game.

"I had a lot of respect for Braase," he said, "but I did well against him today. Sometimes I didn't even know the score, but I knew what it was at the end."

Johnny Sample knew the score every second, and now, as he stood next to the bench where he had meditated five hours earlier, the cornerback opened his wallet and took out a tattered newspa-per clipping. As he unfolded it, the headline blared: KANSAS CITY NOT IN CLASS WITH NFL BEST—LOMBARDI.

"I've saved this since after the first Super Bowl," said Sample, chuckling.

All around him, newsmen were listening to the voice that had antagonized the Colts during the game as he enjoyed his revenge for his *alleged* "blackball" by the NFL.

"It'll take the NFL twenty years to catch us . . .

"They panicked, they were so shaken up, they forgot the game plan, that's why Shula benched Earl Morrall . . .

"Kansas City and Oakland are better than the Colts . . .

"We're the greatest team alive, the greatest team I've ever been on, better than the '58 and '59 Colt teams. . . ."

Nearby, in the crowd around Joe Namath, a man informed the quarterback that he had won a Dodge Charger from *Sport* magazine as the game's "Most Valuable Player."

"Is that one of those I have to give back in a year?"

"No, it's yours," he was told. "It's yours to keep."

"That's more like it," the quarterback said, "but you should give out forty cars, forty-five cars counting the coaches."

"The way things worked out," a newsman asked, "do you feel sorry for Earl Morrall?"

"Better him than me," the quarterback said.

Jimmy "The Greek" Snyder was not convinced. "The Jets did about the same as the other AFL teams had done in the Super Bowl," he was saying in his hospital room. "I mean, they got sixteen points, but their defense was lousy. The thing was, the Colts had their receivers in the end zone, but Morrall missed them. If they played tomorrow, I'd make the Colts the favorite, by 12, like I originally thought."

In the Colt dressing room, a television camera was cloaked. It had been installed there to show their victory celebration, but all the NBC people were in the other dressing room where Commissioner Pete Rozelle was presenting the silver Super Bowl trophy to Phil Iselin. Now, when the Colt players had straggled in, Don Shula looked around.

"The real test of you as individuals," he said, "is yet to come from the abuse and criticism you're going to get."

Soon the newsmen had to be let in—to begin the test that Shula had mentioned. When the door opened and the newsmen started to squeeze through, Tom Matte looked away.

"Oh, no," he moaned.

But among the newsmen was Jack Nicklaus, the golfer who attended Ohio State with the halfback.

"You played a terrific game," Nicklaus said.

"Not good enough to win," Matte replied. "Do you know how sure I was of winning? I was so sure, I'd already spent the money. I'm having an addition built on my home. I'm going to come up seventy-five hundred dollars short of what I planned."

Across the room, Billy Ray Smith, who had hoped to humiliate Joe Namath, was asked about him.

"He gets my vote," the defensive tackle said. "The way he played, he's got to be the best."

"He'd be a superstar in the NFL," agreed Bubba Smith, "but I still can't believe that we lost."

In the trainer's room, Rick Volk was dazed. He hadn't played after being dragged off the field from the pileup on the recovered short kickoff, and now he couldn't remember that kickoff. He didn't even remember the original jolt when Snell flattened him on the game's second play.

"You tackled Snell," said Harry Hulmes, the Colt general manager.

"Did he go down?" Volk asked.

"He went down," Hulmes replied, realizing how really woozy Volk was.

Outside, near his locker, Earl Morrall was surrounded by newsmen.

"I can't account for it," Morrall said. "They made the big plays, and we didn't."

Nearby, staring coldly, Johnny Unitas had been asked if he should have played sooner.

"That's not my decision," he said sharply, "but I was ready to go in at any time. I've been ready for three or four weeks, but that isn't my decision. I haven't had the opportunity to play. You can't change horses in the middle of the stream. The way we were going, it would've been an injustice not to have played Earl. I don't think they're better than us. They stuck to one defense most of the time. That's why I didn't switch our formation, I knew what they would do on defense against that formation. We would've won if I hadn't wasted two minutes down near the goal line before the touchdown."

"How good is Namath?" a newsman inquired.

"Sixteen-to-seven," Johnny Unitas said.

Weeb Ewbank had been tossed into the shower by Gerry Philbin and now, his gray suit still damp, he emerged from the dressing room. Near the entrance, his wife, Lucy, was waiting.

"It was," he told her, "the most satisfying victory of my career."

She knew what he meant. She remembered how the Colts had fired him.

The buses were returning the Jets to the Galt when, in the darkness of the Sunshine State Parkway, an ambulance whizzed by, its red light flashing, its siren howling.

"Hey," yelled Don Maynard, "that ambulance got a dead colt in it."

At the Statler Hilton, the Colts were subdued. Several players, for reasons of protocol, would make an appearance at Carroll Rosenbloom's home, but not Rick Volk and his wife, Charlene. They were in their room with Dr. Norman Freeman, the safetyman sitting on one of the beds, his eyes glazed.

"I'm all right," he was saying.

"Keep him talking," Dr. Freeman told his wife. "Don't let him go to sleep until about midnight. And be sure to report any drowsiness right away."

"Yeah, I'm a little drowsy," Volk said.

"We're all drowsy," the doctor said. "Just keep talking, Rick, keep talking for a few hours."

"I'll keep him talking," Charlene promised.

"Don't hesitate to call," the doctor said.

Moments after the doctor departed, Volk darted into the bathroom. When his wife got to him, he was vomiting as his body heaved and jerked in convulsions. Unconscious, he toppled into the bathtub.

Terrified, his wife screamed. Bolting into the hall, she screamed again. The doctor, who had stopped a few doors away to talk to Dennis Gaubatz, already was on his way back. Seeing the safetyman sprawled unconscious in convulsions, the doctor's first concern was preventing Volk from biting his tongue or swallowing it. Prying open Volk's mouth with his left hand, he used a ballpoint pen to hold the safetyman's tongue flat.

Suddenly, the doctor yanked away his left hand. Volk had bitten the index finger.

Despite the pain and the blood, the doctor resumed his task. The safetyman's body began to relax. Soon he regained consciousness. By that time, Don Shula and Harry Hulmes were in the room. Outside, in the hotel driveway, an ambulance from nearby Holy Cross Hospital slammed to a stop, its siren droning.

At the hospital, Volk was placed under intensive care, but an examination by a neurosurgeon disclosed no serious complications.

The vomiting, according to Dr. Freeman, had increased the intercranial pressure, causing the convulsions. The next day, Rick Volk would feel much better. He would receive flowers from Joe Namath and a phone call from Jim Turner. By Tuesday, he would be discharged. But now, he stirred in his bed and looked up at his wife and the doctor. "Who won the game?" he asked.

The two oldest Talamini children had been at the game and, in their room at the Galt, they were sitting on one of the beds as their father chatted with them.

"Tell me now," he said finally, "what impressed you the most about the game?"

Three-year-old Bobby stared thoughtfully, but silently. Next to him, 5-year-old Robin Marie's face brightened.

"Daddy," she said, "we really socked it to 'em."

Under the blue-and-white tent on Carroll Rosenbloom's lawn, nobody felt like dancing to the music of the six-piece band. Senator Edward Kennedy, a long-time friend of Rosenbloom's, had arrived early and persuaded the Colt owner to go for a swim in the surf. Vice-President Spiro Agnew, once the Governor of Maryland, was there. So was Commissioner Pete Rozelle.

But an expected guest, the silver Super Bowl trophy, was among the absentees.

Champagne bubbled in the glass being held aloft by Johnny Sample.

"I got it," he announced as Matt Snell approached. "My first drink."

"No good," the fullback roared, noticing the half-full glass. "You've got to have a full glass, and it's got to be from a full bottle."

"This is enough." Sample said.

"No, it isn't," Snell insisted.

The fullback disappeared toward the bar in the Continental Room, where a throng of more than four hundred people had assembled for the Jet victory party. The long buffet table had been set with fried chicken, cold cuts, and salads, but the food was being ignored. The bar was the place to be. The champagne was there. Twenty-two cases were available, and Snell obtained a full bottle for the ceremony of Johnny Sample's first drink.

Wandering through the crowd, Betty Iselin, the wife of the president, appeared astounded.

"We're the champions of the world," she kept repeating, "the champions of the *entire* world."

The emotion was there. In the Galt lobby, Curley Johnson had punted Dotty Hampton's blonde wig to the ceiling, and Mrs. George Sauer, Sr., had wept as she embraced her son. But the impact had not yet sunk in. Nobody realized what the Jets had accomplished. Their victory had been not only an historic upset but another milestone in pro football. More than four decades earlier, Harold "Red" Grange was its missionary in the major cities during a barnstorming tour with the Chicago Bears following his famous college career. In 1940, the Bears proved that the "T" formation was the most potent offense with a 73–0 rout of the Washington Redskins in the NFL championship game. And in 1958, the Colts hypnotized the nation's television viewers in the 23–17 sudden-death victory over the New York Giants that lifted pro football toward its popularity.

"They called that one 'The Greatest Game,'" Weeb Ewbank, the man who coached the Colts that day, was saying now as he held the silver Super Bowl trophy, "but I'll take this one."

In two hours and forty-four minutes, the Jets had deflated the myth of NFL superiority. They had shown, as so many of them liked to say, that "football is football" and that, in the Walt Michaels philosophy, "if you hit, you win." Now, after several of the Jets had spoken at the party, Phil Iselin introduced another.

"Here's a man," Iselin said, "who believed in his team and believed in himself, and he said it."

Joe Namath handed his glass of Johnnie Walker Red to his girl-friend, Suzy Storm, and limped to the microphone.

"There's a whole lot of people changing their minds about us now," he began. "Everybody's come up to me tonight, they say, 'I knew you could do it,' nobody said, 'I didn't think you could do it.' Ain't nothin' but a bird, just another football game. But we didn't win on passing, or running, or defense. We beat Baltimore in every phase of the game. If there ever was a world champion, this is it."

The quarterback limped away, and when the applause stopped, Ewbank moved toward the microphone again.

"One game at a time," he said. "Next is the College All-Star game. We'll probably be underdogs again."

After a quick laugh, most of the guests departed. The party was over. In a few minutes, the Super Bowl trophy would be placed behind the registration desk in the Galt lobby. The next morning, when the official group of Jets returned to New York, the trophy would be left behind.

In the Governor's Suite, a bouquet of red roses awaited Joe Namath's return. Confident that the Colts would win, Lou Michaels had ordered a local florist to deliver them that afternoon as a funereal joke on the quarterback. But ironically, Michaels hadn't realized the omen factor.

Twelve diamonds in the brooch, the number 12 on the Jet quarterback's jersey, the January twelfth date, and now twelve roses in his suite.